بسم الله الرحمن الرحيم

About The Author

The author, who writes under the pen-name HARUN YAHYA, was born in Ankara in 1956. Having completed his primary and secondary education in Ankara, he then studied arts at Istanbul's Mimar Sinan University and philosophy at Istanbul University. Since the 1980s, the author has published many books on political, faith-related and scientific issues. Harun Yahya is well-known as an author who has written very important works disclosing the imposture of evolutionists, the invalidity of their claims and the dark liaisons between Darwinism and bloody ideologies such as fascism and communism.

His pen-name is made up of the names "Harun" (Aaron) and "Yahya" (John), in memory of the two esteemed prophets who fought against lack of faith. The Prophet's seal on the cover of the author's books has a symbolic meaning linked to the their contents. This seal represents the Qur'an, the last Book and the last word of Allah, and our Prophet, the last of all the prophets. Under the guidance of the Qur'an and Sunnah, the author makes it his main goal to disprove each one of the fundamental tenets of godless ideologies and to have the "last word", so as to completely silence the objections raised against religion. The seal of the Prophet, who attained ultimate wisdom and moral perfection, is used as a sign of his intention of saying this last word.

All these works by the author centre around one goal: to convey the message of the Qur'an to people, thus encouraging them to think about basic faith-related issues, such as the existence of Allah, His unity and the hereafter, and to display the decrepit foundations and perverted works of godless systems.

Harun Yahya enjoys a wide readership in many countries, from India to America, England to Indonesia, Poland to Bosnia, and Spain to Brazil. Some of his books are available in English, French, German, Italian, Spanish, Portuguese, Urdu, Arabic, Albanian, Russian, Serbo-Croat (Bosnian), Polish, Malay, Uygur Turkish, and Indonesian, and they have been enjoyed by readers all over the world.

Greatly appreciated all around the world, these works have been instrumental in many people putting their faith in Allah and in many others gaining a deeper insight into their faith. The wisdom, and the sincere and easy-to-understand style employed give these books a distinct touch which directly strikes any one who reads or examines them. Immune to objections, these works are characterised by their features of rapid effectiveness, definite results and irrefutability. It is unlikely that those who read these books and give a serious thought to them can any longer sincerely advocate the materialistic philosophy, atheism and any other perverted ideology or philosophy. Even if they continue to advocate, this will be only a sentimental insistence since these books have refuted these ideologies from their very basis. All contemporary movements of denial are ideologically defeated today, thanks to the collection of books written by Harun Yahya.

There is no doubt that these features result from the wisdom and lucidity of the Qur'an. The author certainly does not feel proud of himself; he merely intends to serve as a means in one's search for Allah's right path. Furthermore, no material gain is sought in the publication of these works.

Considering these facts, those who encourage people to read these books, which open the "eyes" of the heart and guide them in becoming more devoted servants of Allah, render an invaluable service.

Meanwhile, it would just be a waste of time and energy to propagate other books which create confusion in peoples' minds, lead man into ideological chaos, and which, clearly have no strong and precise effects in removing the doubts in peoples' hearts, as also verified from previous experience. It is apparent that it is impossible for books devised to emphasize the author's literary power rather than the noble goal of saving people from loss of faith, to have such a great effect. Those who doubt this can readily see that the sole aim of Harun Yahya's books is to overcome disbelief and to disseminate the moral values of the Qur'an. The success, impact and sincerity this service has attained are manifest in the reader's conviction.

One point needs to be kept in mind: The main reason for the continuing cruelty and conflict, and all the ordeals the majority of people undergo is the ideological prevalence of disbelief. These things can only come to an end with the ideological defeat of disbelief and by ensuring that everybody knows about the wonders of creation and Qur'anic morality, so that people can live by it. Considering the state of the world today, which forces people into the downward spiral of violence, corruption and conflict, it is clear that this service has to be provided more speedily and effectively. Otherwise, it may be too late.

It is no exaggeration to say that the collection of books by Harun Yahya have assumed this leading role. By the Will of Allah, these books will be the means through which people in the 21st century will attain the peace and bliss, justice and happiness promised in the Qur'an.

The works of the author include *The New Masonic Order, Judaism and Freemasonry, Global Freemasonry, Islam Denounces Terrorism, Terrorism: The Ritual of the Devil, The Disasters Darwinism Brought to Humanity, Communism in Ambush, Fascism: The Bloody Ideology of Darwinism, The 'Secret Hand' in Bosnia, Behind the Scenes of The Holocaust, Behind the Scenes of Terrorism, Israel's Kurdish Card, The Oppression Policy of Communist China and Eastern Turkestan, Solution: The Values of the Qur'an, The Winter of Islam and Its Expected Spring, Articles 1-2-3, A Weapon of Satan: Romanticism, Signs from the Chapter of the Cave to the Last Times, Signs of the Last Day, The Last Times and The Beast of the Earth, Truths 1-2, The Western World Turns to God, The Evolution Deceit, Precise Answers to Evolutionists, The Blunders of Evolutionists, Confessions of Evolutionists, The Qur'an Denies Darwinism, Perished Nations, For Men of Understanding, The Prophet Musa, The Prophet Yusuf, The Prophet Muhammad (saas), The Prophet Sulayman, The Golden Age, Allah's Artistry in Colour, Glory is Everywhere, The Importance of the Evidences of Creation, The Truth of the Life of This World, The Nightmare of Disbelief, Knowing the Truth, Eternity Has Already Begun, Timelessness and the Reality of Fate, Matter: Another Name for Illusion, The Little Man in the Tower, Islam and the Philosophy of Karma, The Dark Magic of Darwinism, The Religion of Darwinism, The Collapse of the Theory of Evolution in 20 Questions, Allah is Known Through Reason, The Qur'an Leads the Way to Science, The Real Origin of Life, Consciousness in the Cell, A String of Miracles, The Creation of the Universe, Miracles of the Qur'an, The Design in Nature, Self-Sacrifice and Intelligent Behaviour Models in Animals, The End of Darwinism, Deep Thinking, Never Plead Ignorance, The Green Miracle: Photosynthesis, The Miracle in the Cell, The Miracle in the Eye, The Miracle in the Spider, The Miracle in the G nat, The Miracle in the Ant, The Miracle of the Immune System, The Miracle of Creation in Plants, The Miracle in the Atom, The Miracle in the Honeybee, The Miracle of Seed, The Miracle of Hormone, The Miracle of the Termite, The Miracle of the Human Body, The Miracle of Man's Creation, The Miracle of Protein, The Miracle of Smell and Taste, The Secrets of DNA.*

The author's childrens books are: *Wonders of Allah's Creation, The World of Animals, The Splendour in the Skies, Wonderful Creatures, Let's Learn Our Religion, The World of Our Little Friends: The Ants, Honeybees That Build Perfect Combs, Skillful Dam Builders: Beavers.*

The author's other works on Quranic topics include: *The Basic Concepts in the Qur'an, The Moral Values of the Qur'an, Quick Grasp of Faith 1-2-3, Ever Thought About the Truth?, Crude Understanding of Disbelief, Devoted to Allah, Abandoning the Society of Ignorance, The Real Home of Believers: Paradise, Knowledge of the Qur'an, Qur'an Index, Emigrating for the Cause of Allah, The Character of the Hypocrite in the Qur'an, The Secrets of the Hypocrite, The Names of Allah, Communicating the Message and Disputing in the Qur'an, Answers from the Qur'an, Death Resurrection Hell, The Struggle of the Messengers, The Avowed Enemy of Man: Satan, The Greatest Slander: Idolatry, The Religion of the Ignorant, The Arrogance of Satan, Prayer in the Qur'an, The Theory of Evolution, The Importance of Conscience in the Qur'an, The Day of Resurrection, Never Forget, Disregarded Judgements of the Qur'an, Human Characters in the Society of Ignorance, The Importance of Patience in the Qur'an, General Information from the Qur'an, The Mature Faith, Before You Regret, Our Messengers Say, The Mercy of Believers, The Fear of Allah, Jesus Will Return, Beauties Presented by the Qur'an for Life, A Bouquet of the Beauties of Allah 1-2-3-4, The Iniquity Called "Mockery," The Mystery of the Test, The True Wisdom According to the Qur'an, The Struggle with the Religion of Irreligion, The School of Yusuf, The Alliance of the Good, Slanders Spread Against Muslims Throughout History, The Importance of Following the Good Word, Why Do You Deceive Yourself?, Islam: The Religion of Ease, Enthusiasm and Excitement in the Qur'an, Seeing Good in Everything, How do the Unwise Interpret the Qur'an?, Some Secrets of the Qur'an, The Courage of Believers, Being Hopeful in the Qur'an, Justice and Tolerance in the Qur'an, Basic Tenets of Islam, Those Who do not Listen to the Qur'an, Taking the Qur'an as a Guide, A Lurking Threat: Heedlessness, Sincerity in the Qur'an.*

Copyright © Harun Yahya XXX/ 1999 CE
First Published by Vural Yayıncılık, Istanbul, Turkey in March 1999

First English Edition published in October 1999
Second English Edition published in August 2000
Third English Edition published in August 2002

Published by:
Ta-Ha Publishers Ltd.
1 Wynne Road
London SW9 OBB
United Kingdom

Website: http://www.taha.co.uk
E-Mail: sales@taha.co.uk

By Harun Yahya
Translated By: Mustapha Ahmad
Edited By: Abdassamad Clarke

A catalog record of this book is available from the British Library
ISBN 1 89794099 8

Printed and bound by:
Secil Ofset in İstanbul
Address: Yüzyıl Mahallesi MAS-SIT Matbaacılar Sitesi
4. Cadde No:77 Bağcılar- İstanbul / TURKEY

Website
www.harunyahya.com

THE
TRUTH
OF THE
LIFE
OF THIS
WORLD

What is the life of this world
but play and amusement?
But best is the home in the hereafter,
for those who are righteous.
Will you not then understand?
(Surat al-An'am: 32)

HARUN YAHYA

Ta-Ha Publishers Ltd.
1 Wynne Road London SW9 OBB

To The Reader

The reason why a special chapter is assigned to the collapse of the theory of evolution is that this theory constitutes the basis of all anti-spiritual philosophies. Since Darwinism rejects the fact of creation, and therefore the existence of Allah, during the last 140 years it has caused many people to abandon their faith or fall into doubt. Therefore, showing that this theory is a deception is a very important duty, which is strongly related to the religion. It is imperative that this important service be rendered to everyone. Some of our readers may find the chance to read only one of our books. Therefore, we think it appropriate to spare a chapter for a summary of this subject.

In all the books by the author, faith-related issues are explained in the light of the Qur'anic verses and people are invited to learn Allah's words and to live by them. All the subjects that concern Allah's verses are explained in such a way as to leave no room for doubt or question marks in the reader's mind. The sincere, plain and fluent style employed ensures that everyone of every age and from every social group can easily understand the books. This effective and lucid narrative makes it possible to read them in a single sitting. Even those who rigorously reject spirituality are influenced by the facts recounted in these books and cannot refute the truthfulness of their contents.

This book and all the other works of the author can be read individually or discussed in a group at a time of conversation. Those readers who are willing to profit from the books will find discussion very useful in the sense that they will be able to relate their own reflection and experiences to one another.

In addition, it will be a great service to the religion to contribute to the presentation and reading of these books, which are written solely for the good pleasure of Allah. All the books of the author are extremely convincing. For this reason, for those who want to communicate the religion to other people, one of the most effective methods is to encourage them to read these books.

It is hoped that the reader will take time to look through the review of other books on the final pages of the book, and appreciate the rich source of material on faith-related issues, which are very useful and a pleasure to read.

In these books, you will not find, as in some other books, the personal views of the author, explanations based on dubious sources, styles that are unobservant of the respect and reverence due to sacred subjects, nor hopeless, doubt-creating, and pessimistic accounts that create deviations in the heart.

CONTENTS

Introduction

his woman is in her seventies. Have you ever wondered how somebody her age would assess her life?

If she recalls anything about her life, it is surely that it was a "fleeting life".

She would simply remark that her life has not been a "long" one as she dreamed in her teens it would be. It probably never crossed her mind that one day she would grow so old. Yet now, she is overwhelmed by the fact that she has put seventy years behind her. Earlier in life, she probably never thought that her youth and its desires would pass so quickly.

If she were asked late in life to tell her story, her reminiscences would only make a five or six-hour talk. That is all that remains from what she says was "a long life of seventy years".

The mind of a person, worn out with age, is occupied with many questions. These are actually important questions to consider and answering them truthfully is essential to understanding all aspects of life: "What is the purpose of this life that passes so quickly? Why should I remain positive with all the age-related problems I have? What will the future bring?"

The possible answers to these questions fall into two major categories:

those given by people who trust Allah and those given by disbelievers who do not trust Him.

Someone who does not trust Allah would say, "I spent my life chasing vain pursuits. I have put seventy years behind me, but to tell the truth, I still have not been able to grasp what I lived for. When I was a child, my parents were the centres of my life. I found all happiness and joy in their love. Later in life, as a young woman, I devoted myself to my husband and children. During that time, I set many goals for myself. Yet by the time they were achieved, each of them proved to have been a passing whim. When I rejoiced in my success, I headed towards other goals and they occupied me so that I did not think about the real meaning of life. Now at seventy, in the tranquillity of old age, I try to find out what was the purpose of my past days. Is it that I lived for people of whom I have only dim memories now? For my parents? For my husband whom I lost years ago? Or my children whom I see rarely now that they have their own families? I am confused. The only truth is that I feel close to death. Soon I will die and I will become a faint memory in people's minds. What will happen afterwards? I really have no idea. Even the thought of it is frightening!"

There is surely a reason for why she falls into such hopelessness. That is simply because she cannot comprehend that the universe, all living things and human beings have predetermined purposes to fulfil in life. These purposes owe their existence to the fact that everything has been created. An intelligent person notices that plan, design and wisdom exist in every detail of the infinitely varied world. This draws him to recognition of the Creator. He further concludes that since all living things are not the consequences of a random or mindless process they all serve important purposes. In the Qur'an, the last surviving authentic revealed guide to the true path for humanity, Allah repeatedly reminds us of the purpose of our life, which we tend to forget, and thereby summons us to clarity of mind and consciousness.

> It is He Who created the heavens and the earth in six days when His Throne was on the water, in order to test which of you has the best actions. (Surah Hud: 7)

This verse provides a full understanding of the purpose of life for believers. They know that this life is a place where they are tried and tested by their Creator. Therefore, they hope to succeed in this test and attain the Paradise and hence the good pleasure of Allah.

However, for the sake of clarity, there is an important point to consider: those who believe in the 'existence' of Allah do not necessarily have true faith; they do not put their trust in Allah. Today, many people accept that the universe is the creation of Allah; yet, they little comprehend the impact of this fact upon their lives. Therefore, they do not lead their lives as they should. What these people generally regard as the truth is that Allah initially created the universe but then, they believe, He left it on its own.

Allah, in the Qur'an, addresses this misapprehension in the following verse:

> If you ask them, who it is that created the heavens and the earth, they will certainly say, "Allah". Say: "Praise be to Allah!" But most of them understand not. (Surah Luqman: 25)
>
> If you ask them, who created them, they will certainly say, "Allah." How then are they deluded away (from the truth)? (Surat az-Zukhruf: 87)

Due to this misapprehension, people cannot relate their daily lives to the fact that they have a Creator. That is the basic reason why each individual develops his or her personal principles and moral values, shaped within a particular culture, community and family. These principles actually serve as "life-guides" until death comes. People who adhere to their own values always find comfort in the wishful thinking that any wrong actions will be punished temporarily in Hell. The same rationale suggests that eternal life in paradise will follow this period of torment. Such a mentality unwittingly eases fears of the grievous penalty at the end of life. Some, on the other hand, do not even contemplate this issue. They merely remain heedless of the next world and "make the most of their lives".

However, the above is false and the truth is contrary to what they think. Those who pretend not to be aware of the existence of Allah will fall into deep desperation. In the Qur'an, those people are characterised as follows:

They know but the outer (things) in the life of this world: but of the end of things they are heedless. (Surat ar-Rum: 7)

Surely, little do these people grasp the real face and purpose of this world, and they never think that life in this world is not perpetual.

There are some phrases commonly used by people regarding the shortness of this life: "Make the most of your life while it lasts", "life is short", "one does not live forever" are phrases always referred to in definition of the nature of this world. Yet, these phrases contain an implicit attachment to this life rather than the next. They reflect the general attitude of people to life and death. Having such a strong affection for life, conversations about death are always interrupted with jokes or by raising other subjects thus attempting to alleviate the seriousness of the matter. These interruptions are always on purpose, a deliberate effort to reduce such an important subject to insignificance.

Mortality is surely a grave topic to ponder. Until this moment in his life, it may well be that the person is unaware of the significance of this reality. Yet, now that he has the chance to grasp its importance, he must reconsider his life and his expectations. It is never too late to repent to Allah, and to reorient all one's deeds and the conduct of one's life in submission to the will of Allah. Life is short; the human soul is eternal. During this short period, one should not allow temporary passions to control one. A person should resist temptation and keep himself away from everything that will strengthen his bonds to this world. It is surely unwise to neglect the next world just for the sake of the temporary joys of this one.

Nevertheless, disbelievers who cannot comprehend this fact spend their lives in vain being forgetful of Allah. Moreover, they know that it is impossible to attain these desires. Such people always feel a deep dissatisfaction and want even more of what they currently possess. They have endless wishes and desires. Yet, the world is not an appropriate arena in which to satisfy these desires.

Nothing in this world is perpetual. Time works against both what is good and what is new. No sooner does a brand-new car go out of fashion than another model is designed, manufactured and marketed. Similarly, someone may crave others' stately mansions or opulent houses with more rooms than occupants and with gold-plated fixtures, which once he has seen, he loses interest in his own house and cannot avoid regarding them with envy.

An endless search for the new and better, attaching no value to something once it has been achieved, deprecation of the old and placing all hopes in something new: these are the vicious circles that people have everywhere experienced throughout history. Yet an intelligent person should stop and ask himself for a moment: why is he chasing after temporary ambitions and has he ever gained any benefit from such pursuit? Finally, he should draw the conclusion that "there is a radical problem with this viewpoint." Yet people, lacking this kind of reasoning, continue to chase after dreams they are unlikely to achieve.

Nobody, however, knows what will happen even in the next few hours: at any time one may have an accident, be severely injured, or become disabled. Furthermore, time flies in the countdown to one's own death. Every day brings that predestined day closer. Death surely eradicates all ambitions, greed and desires for this world. Under the soil, neither possessions nor status prevail. Every possession with which we are being stingy, including the body, will also vanish and decay in the earth. Whether one is poor or wealthy, beautiful or ugly, one will be wrapped in a simple shroud one day.

We believe that *The Truth of The Life of This World* offers an explanation regarding the real nature of human life. It is a short and deceptive life in which worldly desires seem fascinating and full of promise, but the truth is otherwise. This book will enable you to perceive your life and all of its realities, and help you reconsider your goals in life, if you want to.

Allah enjoins on believers to warn others about these facts, and calls upon them to live only to fulfil His will, as He says in the following verse:

> Verily, the promise of Allah is true: let not then this present life deceive you.... (Surah Luqman: 33)

The Life of this World

O ur universe is perfectly orderly. Countless billions of stars and galaxies move in their separate orbits yet in total harmony. Galaxies consisting of almost 300 billion stars flow through each other and, to everyone's astonishment, during this gigantic transition no collisions occur. Such order cannot be attributed to coincidence. What is more, the velocities of objects in the universe are beyond the limits of man's imagination. The physical dimensions of outer space are enormous when compared to the measurements we employ on earth. Stars and planets, with masses of billions or trillions of tons, and galaxies, with sizes that can only be grasped with the help of mathematical formulae, all whirl along their particular paths in space at incredible velocities.

For instance, the earth rotates about its axis so that points on its surface move at an average velocity of about 1,670 km an hour. The mean linear velocity of the earth in its orbit around the sun is 108,000 km an hour. These figures, however, only relate to the earth. We encounter tremendously larger figures when we examine dimensions beyond the solar system. In the universe, as systems increase in size, velocities also increase. The solar system revolves around the centre of the galaxy at 720,000 km an hour. The velocity of the Milky Way itself, comprising some 200 billion stars, is 950,000 km an hour. This continual movement is inconceivable. The earth, together with the solar system, each year moves 500 million kilometres away from its location of the previous year.

There is an incredible equilibrium within all this dynamic movement and it reveals that life on earth is based on a very delicate balance. Very slight, even millimetric variations in the orbit of heavenly bodies could result in very serious consequences. Some could be so detrimental that life on earth would become impossible. In such systems in which there is both great equilibrium and tremendous velocities, gigantic accidents may happen at any time. However, the fact that we lead our lives in an ordinary way on this planet makes us forget about the dangers existing in the universe at large. The present order of the universe with the almost negligible number of collisions of which we know, simply makes us think that a perfect, stable and secure environment surrounds us.

People do not reflect very much upon such matters. That is why they never discern the extraordinary web of interlocking conditions that makes life possible on earth nor do they apprehend that understanding the real aim of their lives is so important. They live without even wondering how this vast yet delicate equilibrium ever came to be.

Nevertheless, man is endowed with the capacity to think. Without contemplating one's surroundings conscientiously and wisely, one can never see the reality or have the slightest idea why the world is created and who it is who makes this great order move with such perfect rhythms.

One who ponders these questions and grasps their importance comes face to face with an inescapable fact: the universe we live in is created by a Creator, whose existence and attributes are revealed in everything that exists. The earth, a tiny spot in the universe, is created to serve a significant purpose. Nothing occurs purposelessly in the flow of our lives. The Creator, revealing His attributes, His might and wisdom throughout the universe, did not leave man alone but invested him with a significant purpose.

The reason why man exists on earth is recounted by Allah in the Qur'an as follows:

> He Who created death and life, that He may try which of you is best in deed: and He is the Exalted in Might, Oft-Forgiving. (Surat al-Mulk: 2)
> Verily We created Man from a drop of mingled sperm, in order to try him: So We gave him (the gifts) of hearing and sight. (Surat al-Insan: 2)

So We gave him (the gifts) of hearing and sight. (Surat al-Insan: 2)

In the Qur'an, Allah further makes it clear that nothing is purposeless:

We did not create heaven and earth and everything in between them as a game. If We had desired to have some amusement, We could have found it in Our presence, if We would do (such a thing)! (Surat al-Anbiya: 16-17)

The Secret of the World

Allah indicates the purpose of man in the following verse:

We made everything on the earth adornment for it so that we could test them to see whose actions are the best. (Surat al-Kahf: 7)

In doing so, Allah expects man to remain His devoted servant all through his life. In other words, the world is a place where those who fear Allah and those who are ungrateful to Allah are distinguished from each other. The good and the evil, the perfect and the flawed are side by side in this "setting". Man is being tested in many ways. In the end, the believers will be separated from the disbelievers and attain the Paradise. In the Qur'an it is described thus:

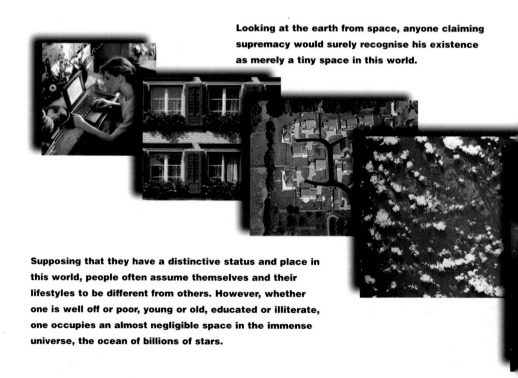

Looking at the earth from space, anyone claiming supremacy would surely recognise his existence as merely a tiny space in this world.

Supposing that they have a distinctive status and place in this world, people often assume themselves and their lifestyles to be different from others. However, whether one is well off or poor, young or old, educated or illiterate, one occupies an almost negligible space in the immense universe, the ocean of billions of stars.

Do people imagine that they will be left to say, 'We believe,' and will not be tested? We tested those before them so that Allah would know the truthful and would know the liars. (Surat al-'Ankabut: 2-3)

In order to have an understanding of the essence of this test, one needs to have a deep understanding of one's Creator whose existence and attributes are revealed in everything that exists. He is the Creator, the Possessor of infinite power, knowledge, and wisdom.

He is Allah – the Creator, the Maker, the Giver of Form. To Him belong the most beautiful names. Everything in the heavens and earth glorifies Him. He is the Almighty, the All-Wise. (Surat al-Hashr: 24)

Allah created man from clay, endowed him with many features, and bestowed many favours upon him. Nobody acquires the traits of seeing, hearing, walking or breathing by himself. Moreover, these complex systems were placed in his body in the womb before he was born and when he was without any ability to perceive the outer world.

Given all these traits, what is expected of man is to be a servant of

The picture indicates the location of the Earth in the Solar System, the location of the Solar System in the Milky Way and finally, the location of our galaxy in the universe.

are "wrongdoers" and "ungrateful" to their Creator, for they refuse submission to Allah. They suppose that life is long and that they possess the individual strength to survive.

That is why their purpose is to "make the most of their lives while they last". They forget death and the hereafter. They endeavour to enjoy life and to attain better living standards. Allah explains the attachment of these people to this life in the following verse:

> As to these, they love the fleeting life, and put away behind them a day (that will be) hard. (Surat al-Insan: 27)

Disbelievers endeavour to taste all the pleasures of this life. Yet, as the verse implies, life passes very quickly. This is the crucial point that the majority of people fail to remember.

Let us think about an example to further clarify the subject.

A Few Seconds or a Few Hours?

Think about a typical holiday: after months of hard work, you have your two weeks' vacation and arrive at your favourite holiday resort after an exhausting eight hours' ride. The lobby is crowded with holidaymakers like you. You even notice familiar faces and greet them. The weather is warm and you do not want to miss one moment enjoying the sunshine and the calm sea, so without losing any time, you find your room, put on your swimsuit and hurry to the beach. At last, you are in the crystal-clear water, but suddenly you are startled by a voice: "Wake up, you will be late for work!"

You find these words nonsense. For a moment, you cannot grasp what is happening; there is an incomprehensible discrepancy between what you see and hear. When you open your eyes and find yourself in your bedroom, the fact that it was all a dream astonishes you greatly. You cannot keep yourself from expressing this astonishment: " I rode eight hours to reach there. Despite the freezing cold outside here today, I felt the sunshine there in my dream. I felt water splashing on my face."

The eight hours' drive to the resort, the time you waited in the lobby, in short everything related to your vacation was actually a dream of a few seconds. Though indistinguishable from real life, what you experienced in a genuine way was merely a dream.

This suggests that we may well be awoken from life on earth just as we are awoken from dream. Then, disbelievers will express exactly the same type of astonishment. In the course of their lives, they could not liberate themselves from the misperception that their lives would be long. Yet, at the time when they will be recreated, they will comprehend that the period of time which appears to have been a lifetime of sixty or seventy years was as if it were merely a few seconds' duration. Allah relates this fact in the Qur'an:

> He will say: "What number of years did you stay on earth?" They will say: "We stayed a day or part of a day: but ask those who keep account." He will say: "You stayed not but a little, if you had only known!" (Surat al-Muminun: 112-114)

Whether it be ten years or a hundred, man will eventually realise the shortness of his life as the verse above relates. This is just like the case of a man who wakes up from dream bitterly witnessing the vanishing of all images of a nice, long holiday, suddenly realising that it had merely been a dream of a few seconds' length. Similarly, the shortness of life will most strike man when all else about his life is forgotten. Allah enjoins careful attention to this fact in the following verse of the Qur'an:

> On the day that the hour (of reckoning) will be established, the transgressors will swear that they tarried not but an hour: thus were they used to being deluded! (Surat or- Rum: 55)

No less than those who live for a few hours or a few days, those who live for seventy years also have a limited time in this world... Something limited is bound to end one day. Be life eighty or a hundred years long, each day brings man closer to that predestined day. Man, in reality, experiences this fact throughout the course of his life. No matter how long-term a plan he devises for himself, one day he attains that specific time when he will accomplish his goal. Every precious objective or thing deemed a turning point in one's life soon turns out merely to have been a passing whim.

Think of a boy, for instance, who recently entered high school. Typically, he cannot wait for the day on which he will graduate. He looks forward to it with unrestrained eagerness. Yet soon he finds himself enrolling in college. At this stage of his life, he does not even recall the long years of high school. He already has other things on his mind; he wants to take advantage of these precious years to ease his fears for the future. Hence, he makes numerous plans. Before long, he becomes busy arranging his forthcoming wedding, a very special occasion that he eagerly awaits. Yet time passes faster than he expected and he leaves many years behind him and finds himself a man supporting a family. By the time he becomes a grandfather, an old man now in declining health, he faintly recalls the events from which he derived pleasure as a young man. Grim memories do fade. The troubles that obsessed him as a young man interest him no more. Only a few images of his life unfurl before his eyes. The appointed time approaches. The time left is very limited; a few years, months or possibly even just days. The classic story of man, without exception, ends here with a funeral service, immediate family members, close friends and relatives attending. The reality is that no man is immune to this end.

Nevertheless, from the beginning of history, Allah has instructed man about the temporary nature of this world and described the Hereafter, his real and eternal residence. Many details pertaining to paradise and hell are depicted in the revelations of Allah. Despite this fact, man tends to forget this essential truth and tries to invest all his efforts in this life, even though it is short and temporary. However only those who assume a rational approach to life are summoned to clarity of mind and consciousness and realise that this life is not worth anything compared to the eternal one. That is why man's objective in life is only to attain paradise, an eternal place of Allah's benevolence and enduring abundance. Seeking the contentment of Allah with true faith is the only way to obtain it. However, those who try not to think about the unavoidable end of this world, and who lead a life in keeping with such an attitude surely deserve eternal punishment.

Allah in the Qur'an relates the awful end that will meet these people:

> One day He will gather them together: (It will be) as if they had tarried but an hour of a day: they will recognise each other: assuredly those will be lost

who denied the meeting with Allah and refused to receive true guidance. (Surah Yunus: 45)

Therefore patiently persevere, as did (all) Messengers of inflexible purpose; and be in no haste about the (disbelievers). On the Day that they see the (punishment) promised them, (it will be) as if they had not tarried more than an hour in a single day. (Yours is but) to proclaim the Message: but shall any be destroyed except those who transgress? (Surat al-Ahqaf: 35)

Unbridled Ambition

Earlier in this book, we mentioned that the time an ordinary man spends in this world is as short as "the blink of an eye". Yet, no matter what a man possesses in life, he does not attain real contentment unless he has faith in Allah and keeps himself occupied with His remembrance.

From the time he begins to become an adult he craves wealth, power or status. To one's astonishment however, he has limited resources to satisfy these cravings; there is no chance whatsoever to possess everything he desires. Neither wealth, nor success nor any form of prosperity, however, will placate his ambitions. Regardless of social status or gender, people's lives are most often limited to six or seven decades only. Upon the termination of this period, death renders all worldly tastes and joys meaningless.

One who is prone to unbridled desires always finds himself incurably "dissatisfied". At every stage of life, this dissatisfaction is always there, while the causes change according to time and conditions. The will to satisfy these desires can make some people indulge in almost anything. He may be so committed to his desires that he is willing to face every consequence, even if it means losing the love of immediate family or being an outcast. Yet by the time he accomplishes his goal, the "magic" disappears. He loses all interest in his accomplished purpose. Moreover, not being content with this accomplishment, he immediately starts to seek another and makes every effort to attain it until he at last achieves it in turn.

Having unbridled ambition is the typical characteristic of a disbeliever. This trait remains with him until he dies. He never feels satisfied with what he possesses. That is because he simply wants everything for his own self-ish greed and not to obtain the contentment of Allah. Likewise, everything people possess and toil to possess is a reason for boasting, and people become heedless of Allah's limits. Surely, Allah will not allow one who is so rebellious against Him to have peace of mind in this world. Allah says in the Qur'anic verse:

> Those who believe and whose hearts find satisfaction in the remembrance of Allah: for, without doubt, in the remembrance of Allah do hearts find satis-faction. (Surat ar-Ra'd: 28)

A Deceptive World

Countless examples of the perfection of the creation surround man all over the world: gorgeous landscapes, millions of different kinds of plants, the blue sky, clouds heavy with rain, or the human body – a perfect organism full of complex systems. These are all breathtaking examples of creation, reflection on which provides deep insight.

Seeing a butterfly displaying its wings, the marvellously intricate patterns of which are statements of its identity, is an experience never to be forgotten. The feathers of a bird's head, so fine and lustrous that they look like rich black velvet, or the attractive colours and scent of a flower are all amazing to the human soul.

Everyone, almost without exception, appreciates a beautiful face. Opulent mansions, gold-plated fixtures and luxury cars for some people are the most cherished possessions. Man craves many other things in life, yet the beauty of whatever we possess is destined to perish in time.

A fruit gradually darkens and finally decays from the moment it is plucked from its branch. The scent of flowers fills our rooms only for a limited period. Soon, their colours fade and they wither away. The prettiest face wrinkles after a few decades: the effect of years on skin and the grey-ing of hairs make that pretty face no different from those of other elderly people. No trace remains of the healthy complexion or ruddy cheeks of a teenager after the passage of years. Buildings need renovation, automobiles become old-fashioned and, even worse, rusty. In brief, everything surrounding us is subject to the ravages of time. This seems to be a "natural process" for some. However, this conveys a clear message: "Nothing is immune to the effects of time."

Above all, every plant, animal, and human being in the world – that is to say, every living thing – is mortal. The fact that the world population does not shrink over the centuries – due to births – should not make us ignore the fact of death.

Yet as an unbridled passion, the spell of possessions and wealth influences man greatly. The lust for possessions unwittingly captures him. However, one point should be grasped: Allah is the sole Owner of everything. Living things remain alive as long as He wills and they die when He decrees their death.

Allah calls upon man to reflect on this in the following verse:

> The likeness of the life of the present is as the rain which We send down from the skies: by its mingling arises the produce of the earth – which provides food for men and animals: (It grows) till the earth is clad with its golden ornaments and is decked out (in beauty): the people to whom it belongs think they have all powers of disposal over it: There reaches it Our command by night or by day, and We make it like a harvest clean-mown, as if it had not flourished only the day before! Thus do We explain the Signs in detail for those who reflect. (Surah Yunus: 24)

In this verse, it is shown that everything on this earth deemed nice and beautiful will lose its beauty one day. Moreover, they will all disappear from the surface of this earth. This is a very important point to ponder since Allah informs us that He gives such examples "for those who think". As an intelligent being, what is expected from man is to think and to take lessons from events and finally to set rational objectives for his life. "Thought" and "comprehension" are the unique traits of man; without these traits man lacks his most distinctive features and becomes lower than the animals. Animals also lead lives which are similar in many respects to human lives: they breathe, breed, and, one day, die. Animals never think why and how they are born, or that they will die one day. It is very natural that they do not engage in an effort to comprehend the real objective of this life; they are not expected to think about the purpose of their creation or about the Creator.

In the Qur'an, the last remaining authentic revelation which guides humanity to the true path, Allah repeatedly reminds us of the temporary nature of this world, summoning us to clarity of mind and consciousness. Indeed, wherever we live, we are all vulnerable to the devastating effects of this world, a self-explanatory phenomenon for people who observe life and the happenings around us. This is also true of all the attractions surrounding us. The pictures in this page are each a demonstration of this fact. Any corner of the world, no matter how impressive, will be exposed to unavoidable deterioration in a few decades, sometimes in even shorter periods of time than one would have ever expected.

Everything on earth is destined to perish. This is the real nature of worldly life...

However, man is responsible to Allah for building consciousness of Allah through pondering on and being mindful of His orders. Furthermore, he is expected to comprehend that this world exists only for a limited period. Those who truly comprehend these facts will seek Allah's guidance and illumination by engaging in good deeds.

Otherwise, man meets suffering both in this world and the Hereafter. He becomes wealthy, but never attains happiness. Beauty and fame usually entail misfortune rather than a joyous life. A celebrity, for instance, who one day basks in the adulation of his fans later battles severe health problems, and one day dies alone in a small hotel room with no-one caring for him.

Qur'anic Examples of the Deception of the World

Allah repeatedly emphasises in the Qur'an that this is just a "world where all pleasures are doomed to perish". Allah tells the stories of those societies and men and women of the past who rejoiced in their wealth, fame or social status yet met disastrous ends. That is exactly what happened to the two men related in Surat al-Kahf:

Set forth to them the parable of two men: for one of them We provided two gardens of grape-vines and surrounded them with date-palms; in between the two We placed corn-fields.

Each of those gardens brought forth its produce, and failed not in the least therein: in the midst of them We caused a river to flow. (Abundant) was the produce this man had: he said to his companion, in the course of a mutual argument: "more wealth have I than you, and more honour and power in (my following of) men."

He went into his garden in a state (of mind) unjust to his soul: He said, "I deem not that this will ever perish, nor do I deem that the Hour (of Judgement) will (ever) come: Even if I am brought back to my Lord, I shall surely find (there) something better in exchange."

His companion said to him, in the course of the argument with him: "Do you deny Him Who created you out of dust, then out of a sperm-drop, then fashioned you into a man? But (I think) for my part that He is Allah, my Lord, and none shall I associate with my Lord. Why did you not, as you went into your garden, say: 'Allah's will (be done)! There is no power but with Allah!' If you see me less than you in wealth and sons, it may be that my Lord will give me something better than your garden, and that He will send on your garden thunderbolts (by way of reckoning) from heaven, making it (but) slippery sand! Or the water of the garden will run off underground so that you will never be able to find it."

So his fruits (and enjoyment) were encompassed (with ruin), and he remained twisting and turning his hands over what he had spent on his property, which had (now) tumbled to pieces to its very foundations, and he could only say, "Woe is me! Would I had never ascribed partners to my Lord and Cherisher!" Nor had he numbers to help him against Allah, nor was he able to deliver himself.

There, the (only) protection comes from Allah, the True One. He is the Best to reward, and the Best to give success. Set forth to them the similitude of the life of this world: It is like the rain which we send down from the skies;

the earth's vegetation absorbs it, but soon it becomes dry stubble, which the winds scatter: it is (only) Allah who prevails over all things. Wealth and sons are allurements of the life of this world, but the things that endure, good deeds, are best in the sight of your Lord as rewards, and best as (the foundation for) hopes. (Surat al-Kahf: 32-46)

Boasting about one's possessions causes a person to be ridiculous. This is the unvarying law of Allah. Wealth and power are given as a gift by Allah and can, at any time, be taken away. The story of "the people of paradise" which is recounted in the Qur'an is another example of this:

Verily We have tried them as We tried the people of the garden, when they resolved to gather the fruits of the (garden) in the morning but made no reservation, ("if it be Allah's Will").Then there came on the (garden) a visitation from your Lord, (which swept away) all around, while they were asleep. So the (garden) became, by the morning, like a dark and desolate spot (whose fruit had been gathered).

As the morning broke, they called out, one to another, "Go you to your tilt (betimes) in the morning, if you would gather the fruits." So they departed, conversing in secret low tones, (saying) "Let not a single indigent person break in upon you into the (garden) this day." And they opened the morning, strong in an (unjust) resolve. But when they saw the (garden), they said: "We have surely lost our way: Indeed we are shut out (of the fruits of our labour)!" Said one of them, more just (than the rest): "Did I not say to you, 'Why not glorify (Allah)?'" They said: "Glory to our Lord! Verily we have been doing wrong!" Then they turned one against another, in reproach. Then some of them advanced against others, blaming each other. They said: "Alas for us! We have indeed transgressed! It may be that our Lord will give us in exchange a better (garden) than this: for we do turn to Him (in repentance)!" Such is the punishment (in this life); but greater is the punishment in the Hereafter, if only they knew! (Surat al-Qalam: 17-33)

The attentive eye immediately recognises from these verses that Allah does not give examples of atheists in this story. The ones in question here are exactly those who believe in Allah but whose hearts have become insensitive towards His remembrance and who are ungrateful to their Creator. They take pride in possessing what Allah gives them as favours, and totally forget that these possessions are only resources to be used in His way. Typically, they affirm the existence and power of Allah; however, their hearts are full of pride, ambition and selfishness.

And coin for them the similitude of the life of the world as water which We send down from the sky, and the vegetation of the earth mingled with it and then became dry twigs that the winds scatter. Allah is able to do all things.
(Surat al-Kahf: 45)

The story of Qarun, one of the people of Moses, is narrated in the Qur'an as an example of the archetypal wealthy worldly character. Both Qarun and those who yearn for his status and wealth are so-called believers who cast their religion away for possessions and thus lose the blessed eternal life, whose loss is eternal deprivation:

Qarun was doubtless of the people of Moses but he acted insolently towards them: such were the treasures We had bestowed on him that their very keys would have been a burden to a body of strong men, behold, his people said to him: "Exult not, for Allah love not those who exult (in riches). But seek, with the (wealth) which Allah has bestowed on you, the Home of the Hereafter, nor forget your portion in this world: but do good, as Allah has been good to you, and seek not (occasions for) mischief in the land: for Allah loves not those who do mischief." He said: "This has been given to me because of a certain knowledge which I have." Did he not know that Allah had destroyed, before him, (whole) generations, which were superior to him in strength and greater in the amount (of riches) they had collected? But the wicked are not called (immediately) to account for their sins. So he went forth among his people in the (pride of his worldly) glitter. Said those whose aim is the life of this world: "Oh! That we had the like of what Qarun has! For he is truly a lord of mighty good fortune!" But those who had been granted (true) knowledge said: "Alas for you! The reward of Allah (in the Hereafter) is best for those who believe and work righteousness: but this none shall attain, save those who steadfastly persevere (in good)." Then We caused the earth to swallow up him and his house; and he had not (the least little) party to help him against Allah, nor could he defend himself. And those who had envied his position the day before began to say on the morrow: "Ah! It is indeed Allah who enlarges the provision or restricts it, to any of His slaves He pleases! Had it not been that Allah was gracious to us, He could have caused the earth to swallow us up! Ah! Those who reject Allah will assuredly never prosper." That home of the hereafter We shall give to those who intend not high-handedness or mischief on earth: and the end is (best) for the righteous. Anyone who does a good action will get something better. As for anyone who does a bad action, those who have done bad actions will only be repaid for what they did. (Surat al-Qasas: 76-84)

The main misdeed of Qarun was to see himself as a separate being apart from and independent of Allah. Indeed, as the verse suggests, he did not deny the existence of Allah, but simply assumed that he – due to his superior traits – deserved the power and wealth bestowed on him by Allah. However, all people in the world are servants of Allah and their posses-

> *The likeness of the life of the present is as the rain which*
> *We send down from the skies: by its mingling arises the*
> *produce of the earth, which provides food for men and*
> *animals: (It grows) till the earth is clad with its golden*
> *ornaments and is decked out (in beauty): the people to*
> *whom it belongs think they have all powers of disposal*
> *over it: There reaches it Our command by night or by day,*
> *and We make it like a harvest clean-mown, as if it had not*
> *flourished only the day before! Thus do We explain the*
> *Signs in detail for those who reflect. (Surah Yunus: 24)*

sions are not given to them simply because they deserve them. Everything given to man is the favour of Allah. If he is aware of this fact, man will not become ungrateful and spoilt towards his Creator due to the riches in his possessions. He will only feel grateful and show this gratitude by his good manners towards Allah. This is certainly the best and most honourable way of showing one's gratitude to Allah. On the other hand, Qarun and those who aspire to be like Qarun realise the wicked deeds they engage in only when a disaster falls upon them. After all the harm that befalls them, if they persist and still revolt against Allah, they are utterly ruined. Their end will be unavoidable: the Hell, an evil place in which to remain!

> Know you (all), that the life of this world is but play and amusement, pomp and mutual boasting and multiplying (in rivalry) among yourselves, riches and children. Here is a similitude: How rain and the growth which it brings forth delight (the hearts of) the tillers; soon it withers; you will see it grow yellow; then it becomes dry and crumbles away. But in the Hereafter is a Penalty severe (for the devotees of wrong). And Forgiveness from Allah and (His) Good Pleasure (for the devotees of Allah). And what is the life of this world, but goods and chattels of deception? (Surat al-Hadid: 20)

The Weaknesses of Man

llah created man in a most complete state and equipped him with superior characteristics. His superiority over all creatures – as shown by his distinctive intellectual skills of thought and comprehension, and his readiness to learn and develop cultures – is unquestionable.

Have you ever thought why it is that despite all these superior features man has such a fragile body, which is always vulnerable to external and internal threat? Why is it exposed to the attacks of microbes or bacteria, which are so tiny they are invisible to the naked eye? Why does he have to spend a certain part of each day keeping himself clean? Why does he need bodily care? And why does he age in the course of time?

People assume that these needs are natural phenomena. Yet, being in need of care as a human serves a special purpose. Every detail of the needs of man is specially created. The verse **"man was created weak"** (Surat an-Nisa: 28) is the manifest statement of this fact.

Man's infinite needs are created on purpose: to make him understand that he is a servant of Allah and that this world is a temporary residence for him.

Man has no influence whatsoever on the date and place of his birth. Likewise, he never knows where or how he will die. Moreover, all his efforts to eliminate the factors negatively affecting his life are vain and hopeless.

Man has indeed a fragile nature requiring a lot of care to survive. He is intrinsically unprotected against, and feeble in the face of, abrupt and unforeseeable incidents that occur in the world. Equally, he is exposed to unpredictable health risks, no matter whether he is a resident of a high civilisation or of a remote, undeveloped mountain village. It is quite likely that at any moment man can develop an incurable or fatal disease. At any time, an accident may happen dealing unrecoverable harm to one's bodily strength or one's most enviable charms. Furthermore, this applies to all people: status, rank and race, etc., know of no exception to such an end. Both the life of a celebrity with millions of fans and that of a common shepherd may well be completely altered one day by an unexpected incident.

The human body is a weak organism of bones and flesh averaging 70-80 kilograms in weight. Only a frail skin protects it. No doubt, this sensitive skin can easily be hurt and bruised. It becomes cracked and dry when exposed to too much sunlight or wind. In order not to surrender to natural causes man always has to be on guard against the effects of the environment.

Although man is equipped with marvellous bodily systems, the "materials" – the flesh, muscles, bones, nervous tissue, cardiovascular system and fat – are prone to decay. If man were of a different material, rather than flesh and fat, a material that gave no access to external intruders such as microbes or bacteria, there would be no chance of becoming sick. However, flesh is the frailest 'substance': it becomes rotten and even worm-eaten when left at room temperature for some time.

As a constant reminder of Allah, man often feels the fundamental needs of his body. Exposed to cold weather, for instance, he runs health risks; his immune system gradually "collapses". On such an occasion, his body may fail to maintain the constant body temperature (37^0C) that is fundamental to good health.[1] His heart rate slows, the blood vessels contract, and arterial pressure increases. The body starts to shiver as a means of regaining heat. A lowered body temperature of 35^0C accompanied by a depressed pulse and contracted blood-vessels in arms, legs and fingers signals a life-threatening condition.[2] A person with a body temperature of 35^0C suffers severely from disorientation and constantly falls asleep. Mental functions slow. A slight decrease in body temperature can cause such consequences, but even more exposure to cold weather, bringing body temperature below 33^0C, causes loss of consciousness. At 24^0C, the respiratory system fails to function. The brain is damaged at 20^0C and finally the heart stops at 19^0C bringing on the unavoidable end: death.

This is only one of the examples upon which will be further expanded in the remaining pages of this book. The purpose in providing these examples is to emphasise that, due to the inexorable factors endangering his being, man will always fail to find profound satisfaction in his way of living. The aim is to remind the reader that man should avoid blind attachment to life and stop spending all his life running after dreams and, instead, always remember Allah and the real life, the Hereafter.

There is an eternal Paradise promised to man. As readers will have the opportunity to see from the pages that follow, paradise is a place of perfection. In paradise, man will be entirely insulated from all the physical weaknesses and imperfections that surround him on earth. Everything he desires will be within easy reach. Furthermore, fatigue, thirst, exhaustion, hunger, and injury do not exist in paradise.

Helping people reflect on their real nature and consequently have a deeper understanding of the infinite superiority of the Creator is another purpose of this book. In addition, comprehending that man is in need of the guidance of Allah is surely of great relevance to everyone. Allah states this in the following verse:

> O mankind! You are the poor in your relation to Allah. And Allah! He is the Absolute, the Owner of Praise. (Surah al-Fatir: 15)

Bodily Needs

Man is exposed to many physical risks. Keeping one's body and environment clean and taking painstaking care of them are life-long burdens with which one has always to be occupied in order to minimise health risks. What is even more striking is that the amount of time spent on such tasks is considerable. We have often come across surveys that have been conducted to find out how much time is spent shaving, bathing, hair-care, skin-care, manicuring etc. The results of such surveys are astounding, and reveal how much precious time such daily tasks consume.

In the course of our lives, we encounter many people. At home, in the office, on the streets or in the shopping-mall, we see many smartly dressed people in their best states. They are people with shaved faces, clean hair and bodies, ironed shirts, well-polished shoes. However, such careful grooming requires time and effort.

From the moment one wakes up in the morning until the time one goes to sleep, one has to involve oneself in endless routines to keep clean and fresh. Once we wake up, the first place we head for is the bathroom; during the night, the proliferation of bacteria causes a bad taste and unpleasant odour in the month, forcing us to brush our teeth immediately. However, in order to get ready for the new day, the essentials are not limited to brushing teeth. Neither does washing just the face and hands suffice. During the day, hair becomes greasy and the body becomes dirty. At night, in the midst of a dream, it might not be possible to stop sweating. As the only way to get rid of unpleasant body odours and sweat, one feels the urgent need of a shower. Otherwise, it would not be pleasant to go to work with greasy hair and a bad odour coming from the body.

The variety of materials used to make one's body clean enough to face others is surprisingly wide. This is, surely, enough evidence of the body's endless needs. Besides water and soap, we need numerous essentials to clean the body: shampoo, conditioner, toothpaste, tooth polish, dental tape, cotton buds, body powder, face cream, lotions; the list goes on and on. Apart from these essentials, there are hundreds of other products developed in laboratories to enhance body care.

As well as bodily care, everyone must also spend a considerable amount of time cleaning clothing, house, and surroundings. No doubt, one cannot keep oneself clean unless one is in a clean environment.

In brief, a certain part of life is spent solely to provide for the needs of the body. Moreover, we need many chemicals for this end. Allah created man with many weaknesses, yet He also provides the methods to temporarily conceal these weaknesses and hence remain in good condition without making other people conscious of these weaknesses. Besides, man is endowed with intelligence enough to find the best ways to cover his "weaknesses". If we neglect to apply these methods staying clean and fresh, we may in a very short time begin to appear repulsive.

Furthermore, one cannot remain clean for a long time. After a few hours, nothing remains from the refreshment a shower gives: we can only stay clean for a relatively short time. We need to take a shower at least once a day. Likewise, we need to brush our teeth regularly: bacteria quickly turn the mouth into its former state. A woman who spends hours in front of a mirror putting on make-up wakes up next morning with no trace of that beautiful make-up on her face. Moreover, if she does not remove it properly, her face may look even worse due to the remains of cosmetics. A clean-shaven man needs another shave the next morning.

It is important to understand that all these needs are created for a specific purpose. An example makes this point explicit: when body temperature rises, we sweat. The odour accompanying sweat is disturbing. This is an unavoidable process for anyone living in this world. However, this need not have been the case! For instance, plants never sweat. A rose never stinks despite the fact that it grows in soil, is fed with manure, and remains in an environment of dust and dirt. Under all conditions, it has a delicate fragrance. We need hardly mention that it needs no body-care! However, no matter which cosmetics are applied to the skin, few human beings can achieve such a permanent fragrance.

Besides all the needs of the body pertaining to hygiene, nutrition is also essential for health. There is a delicate balance of proteins, carbohydrates, sugars, vitamins and various minerals essential for the body. Once this balance is impaired, serious damage may arise in the functioning of bodily systems: the immune system loses its protective abilities, leaving the body weak and exposed to disease. Therefore, the same attention shown to body-care should also be paid to nutrition.

An even more essential requisite for life is, of course, water. A man can survive without food for a certain period, but a few days without water will have fatal consequences. All the chemical functions of the body take place with the aid of water; water is vital for life.

The foregoing are the weaknesses that one can observe in one's own body. Yet a question remains: are we all aware that these are weaknesses? Alternatively, do we think that these are 'natural' since human beings all over the world have such weaknesses? However, we should keep in mind that Allah could have created man perfect without any of these weaknesses. Each human being could have been as clean and as fragrant as a rose. Nevertheless, the lessons drawn from such a state lead eventually to wisdom, summoning us to clarity of mind and consciousness; man, seeing his weaknesses in the presence of Allah, should understand why he is created and try to lead an honourable life as a servant of Allah.

Fifteen Years Without "Consciousness"

Everyone has to spend some of his daily time sleeping. No matter how much work he has or how he struggles to avoid it, it is inescapable that he will fall asleep and remain in bed for at least a quarter of the day. Hence, man is conscious only eighteen hours a day; he spends the remaining time – a minimum of six hours a day on average – in complete unconsciousness. When assessed from this standpoint, we come across a striking picture: one quarter of an average 60 years of life is spent in total unconsciousness.

Do we then have an alternative to sleep? What would happen to someone who said, "I do not want to sleep?"

First, one's eyes become red and one's skin colour pales. If the duration of sleeplessness extends, loss of consciousness results.

Closing the eyes and the inability to focus attention are the initial phases of falling asleep. This is an inevitable process, and beautiful or ugly, wealthy or poor, everybody experiences the same process.

Similarly to death, just before sleep the body starts to become insensitive to the outer world and gives no response to any stimulus. Senses that were exceptionally keen a while ago start to fail. In the meantime, perceptions are altered. The body reduces all functions to a minimum, leading to disorientation in place and time and slower body movements. This state is, in a way, a different form of death, which is defined as the state in which the soul leaves the body. Indeed, while sleeping the body lies in bed where the spirit experiences totally different lives in completely different places. In one's dreams, one may well perceive oneself on a beach on a hot summer's day, unaware that one is sleeping in bed. Death, too, has the same outward appearance: it separates the soul from the body which the soul uses in this world and carries him away to another world in a new body. For this reason, Allah, in the Qur'an, the only remaining authentic revelation which guides humanity to the true path, repeatedly reminds us of the similarity of sleep to death.

> It is He who takes your souls by night, and has knowledge of all that you have done by day: by day He raises you up again; that a term appointed be fulfilled; In the end unto Him will be your return; then will He show you the truth of all that you did. (Surat al-An'am: 60)
>
> It is Allah that takes the souls (of men) at death; and those that die not (He takes) during their sleep: those on whom He has passed the decree of death, He keeps back, but the rest He sends (to their bodies) for a term appointed. Verily in this are Signs for those who reflect. (Surat az-Zumar: 42)

Totally deprived of all the functions of the senses, in other words, "in a dead faint", a person spends up to a third of his life in sleep. Yet, he little contemplates this fact, never realising that he leaves behind everything deemed important in this world. An important exam, huge sums of money lost on the stock exchange or a minor personal problem, in brief everything that appears to be of crucial importance during the day fades away as one falls asleep. This simply means having no relationship with the world at all.

All the examples that have been presented so far give a clear idea about the shortness of life and the huge amount of time spent on "compulsory" routine tasks. When the time spent on such "compulsory" tasks is subtracted, one realises the scarcity of moments left for the so-called joys of life. In retrospect, one feels astonished at the long time spent on nourishment, body-care, sleep, or working to attain better standards of living.

The calculations of the time spent on routine tasks necessary for survival are, undoubtedly, worth thinking about. As stated earlier, at least 15-

20 years of a 60-year life are spent asleep. The initial 5-10 years of the remaining 40-45 years, however, are spent in childhood, another period that is also spent in an almost unconscious state. In other words, a sixty-year-old man will have spent perhaps half of his life without consciousness. Regarding the other half of life, many statistics are available. These figures, for instance, include the time spent preparing meals, eating, bathing or caught in traffic jams. This list can be further extended. In conclusion, what remains from a "long" life is only 3-5 years. What is the importance of such a short life in comparison to an eternal one?

It is right at this point that a huge gulf yawns between those who have faith and disbelievers. Disbelievers, believing the only life to be here on this earth, struggle to make the most of it. Yet these are useless endeavours: this world is both short and its life is beset with "weaknesses". Furthermore, since the disbeliever does not put his trust in Allah, he lives a troublesome life, one fraught with concerns and fears.

Those who have faith, on the other hand, spend their lives remembering Allah and in His presence at each instant, during all of the minor and troublesome occupations of bodily care, eating, drinking, standing, sitting, reclining to sleep, and seeking livelihoods, etc. They spend their lives only to attain the contentment of Allah and thus lead peaceful lives, isolated completely from all worldly sorrows and fears. In conclusion, they attain paradise, a place of eternal happiness. Similarly, the ultimate purpose of life is stated in the verse:

> To the righteous (when) it is said, "What is it that your Lord has revealed?" they say, "All that is good." To those who do good, there is good in this world, and the home of the hereafter is even better and excellent indeed is the home of the righteous. (Surat an-Nahl: 30-31)

Disease and Accidents

Disease also reminds man how prone he is to weakness. The body, highly protected against all types of external threats, is seriously affected by mere viruses, disease-producing agents invisible to the naked eye. This process seems unreasonable, since Allah equipped the body with very complete systems, especially the immune system that could be described as a "victorious army" over its enemies. However, despite the body's strengths and defences, people often fall ill. They little ponder the fact that having been equipped with such excellent systems, Allah might never have allowed disease-producing agents to cause suffering. Viruses, microbes or bacteria might never have affected the body, or these tiny "enemies" might never have existed. However, still today, anyone may well become the target of serious disease arising from insignificant causes. For instance, a single virus entering the body through a slight cut on the skin may in a short while spread to the whole body, taking control of vital organs. Despite advanced technology, a simple influenza virus may become a life-threatening factor for huge numbers of people. History has frequently been witness to influenza cases that changed even the demographic structures of countries. For instance, in 1918, twenty-five million people died of influenza. Similarly, in 1995, an epidemic claimed thirty thousand lives, the worst losses concentrated in Germany.

Today the danger persists: a virus may strike at any time and easily become life-threatening for anyone, or a rare disease may reappear after lying dormant for nearly twenty years. Accepting all these incidents as natural happenings and not reflecting on them would be a serious mistake. Allah gives mankind diseases for a special purpose. This way, those who are arrogant may well find an opportunity to grasp the truly limited extent of their power. Besides, this is a good way of understanding the true nature of this life.

Apart from diseases, accidents pose serious threats to man. Every day newspapers run headlines about traffic accidents. Accidents also constitute a considerable part of radio and television news. Yet, despite such familiarity with accidents, we never think we might face an accident at any moment. There are thousands of factors around us that may suddenly divert the flow of our lives. One may lose one's balance and fall in the middle of the street, for instance. A haemorrhage in the brain or a broken leg may well be traced back to such an ordinary accident, or while eating supper, one may choke to death on a fish-bone. The causes may sound simple, but every day thousands of people around the world face incidents such as these which are difficult to imagine.

These facts should make us understand the futility of devotion to this world and conclude that everything that has been given us is but a temporary favour to test us in this world. It is unfathomable how a human being, still unable to combat an invisible virus, dares to display arrogance towards his Almighty Creator.

No doubt, it is Allah who created man and He is the One who protects him against all dangers. In this respect, accidents and disease show us who we are. No matter how potent one assumes oneself to be, except by the will of Allah, one cannot prevent any disaster from befalling. Allah creates all disease and other situations to remind man of his weaknesses.

This world is a place to test man. Everyone is held responsible for trying to attain His good pleasure. At the end of this test, those who have a clear unitary knowledge of Allah without ascribing partners to Him and obey His prohibitions and orders will reside in paradise for all eternity. Those who do not change their arrogance and prefer this world and their desires will thus lose an eternal life of bliss and ease in exchange for eternal suffering and will never be free of troubles, weakness and sorrow either in this world or in the Hereafter.

The Consequences of Diseases and Accidents

As stated earlier, disease and accidents are the events by which Allah tests man. Facing such an incident, a faithful person immediately turns to Allah, praying and seeking refuge in Him. He is well aware that nothing and no-one except Allah can save him from grief. He is also aware that his patience, devotion and trust in Allah are being tested. In the Qur'an, the prophet Ibrahim is praised for his exemplary attitude. His sincere prayer is one that should be repeated by all believers. It is related in the Qur'an as follows:

> "…Who gives me food and drink, and when I am ill, it is He who cures me; Who will cause me to die, and give me life (again)." (Surat ash-Shu'ara: 79-81)

The prophet Ayub, on the other hand, set a good example for all believers as he sought patience only from Allah when faced with a bitter illness:

> Commemorate Our slave Ayyub. Behold he cried to his Lord: "The Evil One has afflicted me with distress and suffering!" (Surah Sad: 41)

Such distress strengthens the loyalty of believers towards their Creator and establishes them in maturity. That is why each suffering is a "fortune". Disbelievers, on the other hand, perceive all types of accident and disease as "misfortune". Not realising that everything is created for a specific purpose and that patience shown during troubles will be awarded in the Hereafter, disbelievers fall into great grief. Indeed, since in a system based upon the denial of the existence of Allah, people adopt a materialistic standpoint, disease and accidents bring other sorrows to those who have no faith. The moral values and point of view of materialist society dictates that after accident or disease what they generally experience is the sudden disappearance of close 'friends' even if they have not died. Such an attitude is assumed simply because they perceive being friends with, or taking care of a sufferer as trouble. No matter how much love and care he gave in the "good old days", once somebody becomes ill – bedridden for instance – or disabled, all affection felt for him vanishes. Another reason which makes people change is the loss of looks or of certain skills. That is also what is expected from materialist society, since in such a society, people assess others according to their physical traits. Consequently, when a physical defect appears, the value attached to that person also diminishes.

For instance, the spouse or close relatives of a physically handicapped person, immediately start complaining about the difficulties of looking after a disabled person. They often lament about how unfortunate they are. Most express that they are still very young and that being faced with such a disaster is not something they deserve. This is only self-justification for why he or she does not pay proper care and attention to his or her disabled relative. Some, on the other hand, assist the patient or disabled just because they fear what others might think about them in the event that they leave them. The rumours, which are likely to spread, simply prevent them from such behaviour. In such times of trouble the promises of loyalty given during happier days are suddenly replaced by egotistical, selfish feelings.

Such incidents should not surprise us in a society where some forms of behaviour, such as loyalty, are only shown when there is benefit to be derived from them. No doubt, in a society where materialistic criteria are well established and, more importantly, where people have no fear of Allah, it is impossible to expect someone to remain loyal to somebody else for no price. After all, we cannot expect someone to be sincere and honest to others unless he believes he will receive punishment in return for his failure to act so or reward for doing so. Such behaviour is believed to be "idiotic" in materialist society. That is because there is no sense in showing loyalty to someone who will, when death befalls him possibly in a few decades, cease to exist for all eternity. Considering the situation in a system in which both parties are convinced they will live for a short time then die, such a mentality seems reasonable. Why, then, should they not prefer the comfortable and easy way of doing things?

Yet, the facts are otherwise. Those who trust Allah, who, in His presence, are aware of their weaknesses and fear Him, assess other people in the way Allah wants them to. The most precious feature of a person who is in the presence of Allah is his fear, respect and, hence, the noble behaviour he displays arising from these qualities. If the one who fears Allah dis-

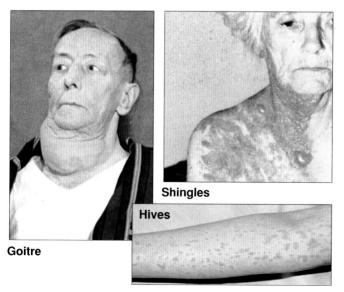

Goitre

Shingles

Hives

Diseases, such as those that are illustrated next, are often trials from Allah. Such incidents are rare opportunities for believers to show their patience and devotion to Allah. Yet, those who limit their understanding to this world alone hardly comprehend this essential secret.

plays moral perfection in this world, he will attain physical and mental perfection for all eternity. Knowing this fact, the physical defects of this world lose all significance. This is the promise of Allah to the believers. That is also the basic reason why believers show respect and affection to each other and consideration for each other's physical handicaps, and demonstrate lifelong devotion to one another.

This big gap in perception between believers and disbelievers and the different states of mind they experience are quite important. While grudges and anger are eliminated from the hearts of believers and peace and security prevail instead, feelings of disappointment, dissatisfaction and unhappiness create anguished states of mind for disbelievers. This is as if it was a punishment from the materialist society surrounding the disbelievers, but, it really is a misfortune from Allah for those who do not believe. Those who assume that they will not be judged for their misdeeds will be stunned on the day of judgement when their misdeeds – cruelty, disbelief, and disloyalty – will be judged:

> Let not the disbelievers think that Our respite to them is good for them: We grant them respite that they may grow in their iniquity: But they will have a shameful punishment. (Surat Ali-'Imran: 178)

The Later Years of Life

The destructive effects of the passage of years are observable in one's own body. As the years go by, the body, the most precious possession a human being has, goes through an irreversible process of destruction. The changes a human being experiences throughout his life are recounted in the Qur'an as follows:

> It is Allah Who created you in a state of (helpless) weakness, then gave (you) strength after weakness, then, after strength, gave (you) weakness and a hoary head: He creates as He wills, and it is He who has all knowledge and power. (Surat ar-Rum: 54)

The later years of life are the times most neglected in the future plans of an adult, except in the anxious process of saving for old-age pensions. Indeed, being too close to death, people usually develop a hesitant approach to this period. When someone tries to talk about old age, others feel concerned and attempt to change this "unpleasant" topic as soon as possible. The routine of daily life is also a good way of escaping from the thought of these potentially miserable years of life. So, it is postponed until the day one inevitably meets it. No doubt, the main reason for such avoidance is the assumption that one has endless time until death comes upon one. This common misconception is described in the Qur'an:

> Nay, We gave the good things of this life to these men and their fathers until life grew long for them. (Surat al-Anbiya: 44)

This mistaken idea often leads to great grief. That is simply because, no matter how old one is, the only real possessions remaining from one's past are dimly-recalled memories. One barely remembers childhood. It is even hard to recall exactly what happened during the last decade. The greatest ambitions of a young man, important decisions, and the goals to which he is most committed, all lose their significance once they are experienced and done. That is why to tell a "long" life story is a vain endeavour.

Whether a teenager or an adult, this should prompt man to make an important decision about his life. For instance, if you are forty and expect to live until your mid-sixties – and of that you have no guarantee – those remaining twenty-five years will surely pass as quickly as the preceding forty years. The same holds true even if your life is prolonged a great deal, since the remaining thirty or forty years will, likewise, pass before you even notice. This is, surely, a perpetual reminder of the true nature of this world. One day every living soul on this earth will leave this world and there is no return.

Hence, man should set aside his prejudices and be more realistic about his life. Time passes very quickly and each day brings on further physical weakness and more impaired thinking rather than fresher dynamism and a younger figure. In brief, growing old is a manifestation of man's inability to control his own body, life and destiny. Time's adverse effects on the body become visible during this period. Allah informs us about this in the following verse:

> It is Allah Who creates you and takes your souls at death; and of you there are some who are sent back to a feeble age, so that they know nothing after having known (much): for Allah is All-Knowing, All-Powerful. (Surat an-Nahl: 70)

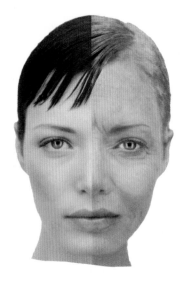

In medicine, advanced old age is also called "the second childhood". Hence, during this latter stage of life, elderly people just like children need care, since their bodily and mental functions go through certain alterations.

As one grows older, physical and spiritual characteristics pertaining to childhood become more apparent. Elderly people fail to do many tasks requiring physical strength. Changes in judgement, impaired thinking, difficulties in walking, maintaining balance and speech, impediments, memory impairment and gradual memory loss, and changes in mood or behaviour are only a few symptoms of diseases commonly seen in old age.

In short, after a certain period, people often regress to a state of childish dependency both physically and mentally.

Life both begins and ends in an infant-like state. This is evidently not a random process. It is possible that man could remain young until he dies. Yet Allah reminds man about the temporary nature of this world by making the quality of his life deteriorate at certain stages of life. This process serves as a clear reminder that life is slipping away. Allah explains this matter in the verse below:

> O mankind! If you have doubt about the Resurrection, (consider) that We created you out of dust, then out of a drop, then out of a leech-like clot, then out of a morsel of flesh, partly formed and partly unformed, in order that We may manifest (Our power) to you; and We cause whom We will to rest in the wombs for an appointed term, then We bring you out as babes, then (foster you) that you may reach your age of full strength; and some of you are called to die, and some are sent back to the feeblest old age, so that they know nothing after having known (much), and (further), you see the earth barren and lifeless, but when We pour rain down on it, it is stirred (to life), it swells, and it puts forth every kind of beautiful growth (in pairs). (Surat al-Hajj: 5)

Age-related Physical Problems

No matter how much money you have or how good your health, every-one eventually faces disabilities and other age-related complications, some of which are described below:

Skin is truly an important factor determining how somebody looks. It is an essential component of beauty. When tissue of a few square millimetres is removed, one inevitably comes across a picture which squeamish people find disturbing. This is solely because, apart from offering protection from exterior threats to the body, skin also provides a smooth and aesthetic appearance to the body. This is, no doubt, quite an important function of skin. After all, if someone assumes herself good looking, that is solely because her skin, a piece of flesh weighing in total around four and a half pounds, covers her body. Yet to one's astonishment, this is the only organ that becomes visibly damaged when one gets old.

As one grows old, skin loses its elastic structure since structural proteins making up the "skeleton" of its bottom layers become sensitive and weak. That is also why wrinkles and lines, a nightmare for many people, appear on the face. The functioning of the oil glands in the top layer of the skin slows down, causing acute dryness. In time, the body is exposed to external influences since the permeability of skin increases. As a result of this process, elderly people suffer seriously from sleeping disorders, superficial wounds, and an itch called "the itch of old age". Likewise, damage occurs to the bottom layers of the skin. Renewal of skin tissue and substance-exchange mechanisms fail to function to a great extent, preparing and laying the ground for tumours to develop.

Strength of bones is also of great importance to the human body. Efforts to achieve an erect posture rarely meet with success for old people, while it is much easier for the young. Walking with a bent posture, one loses all one's loftiness and arrogance, giving the message that one no longer has the ability to exercise control even over one's own body. Therefore, this is also a loss of one's "airs and graces".

The symptoms of ageing are not limited to these alone. Elderly people are more likely to develop loss of sensation since nerve cells cease to

(Above) Jeanne Calment, the oldest French woman. There is a period of a century between these two photographs.
(Middle) Naty Revuelta, in youth and old age.

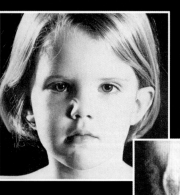

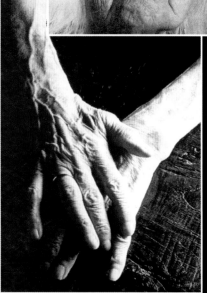

(Below) Everybody experiences the changes seen in these pictures. The process of ageing is the clearest evidence that we are living in a temporary world. Man comes into this world, grows to adulthood and old age and then dies. Yet, only the body experiences this irreversible process. The soul, on the other hand, lives forever.

renew themselves after a particular age. Elderly people suffer from spatial disorientation due to weakening eyes in response to the intensity of light. This is quite important since it means a limitation of eyesight: the vividness of colours, the positions of objects, and their dimensions become blurred. These are, no doubt, difficult situations for the elderly to adapt to.

Man might never have experienced the physical destruction of ageing: he might simply have grown stronger and healthier as he grew older. Though we are not familiar with such a model, living longer might have offered unprecedented opportunities for personally and socially fulfilling lives. Time might have improved the quality of life, making it much more enjoyable than ever. Yet, the system ordained as good for mankind is one based on a declining quality of life as one grows older.

This is one more evidence of the temporary nature of this world. Allah repeatedly reminds us of this fact in the Qur'an and commands believers to think about it:

> The likeness of the life of the present is as the rain which We send down from the skies: by its mingling arises the produce of the earth – which provides food for men and animals: (It grows) till the earth is clad with its golden ornaments and is decked out (in beauty): the people to whom it belongs think they have all powers of disposal over it: There reaches it Our command by night or by day, and We make it like a harvest clean-mown, as if it had not flourished only the day before! Thus do We explain the Signs in detail for those who reflect. (Surah Yunus: 24)

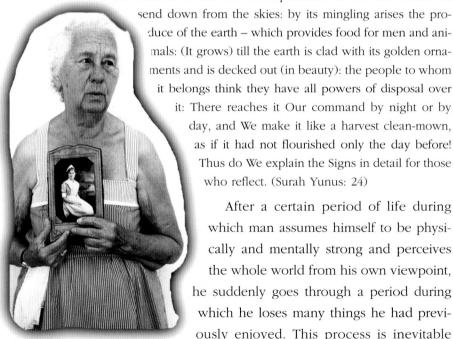

The picture this old lady holds in her hand is one of her youth.

After a certain period of life during which man assumes himself to be physically and mentally strong and perceives the whole world from his own viewpoint, he suddenly goes through a period during which he loses many things he had previously enjoyed. This process is inevitable and irreversible. That is only because Allah created this world as a temporary place in which to live and made it imperfect in order that it serve as a reminder for the Hereafter.

Lessons to be Drawn from the Old Age of Celebrities

Growing old is unavoidable. Nobody, without exception, can escape it. Yet seeing celebrities becoming older has a deeper influence on us since their physical deterioration is openly observable. Witnessing the ageing of people renowned for their fame, wealth and beauty is surely a reminder of the shortness and insignificance of this life.

Every day it is possible to observe this fact from hundreds of examples around us. An intelligent, healthy and famous person, once a symbol of beauty or success, one day appears in newspapers, magazines and on television with a physical or mental disability. This is the end that almost everybody will meet. Yet celebrities hold a special place in our minds; the way they grow old and lose their charms appeals to the emotions more deeply. In the pages that follow, you will see photographs of some celebrities. Each one is the clearest evidence that no matter how beautiful, successful or young you are, the inevitable end for human beings is old age.

The Death of Man

Life slips away second by second. Are you aware that every day brings you closer to death or that death is as close to you as it is to other people?

As we are told in the verse "Every soul shall taste death in the end; to Us shall you be brought back." (Surat al-'Ankabut: 57) everyone who has ever appeared on this earth was destined to die. Without exception they all died, every one. Today, we hardly come across the traces of many of these people who passed away. Those currently living and those who will ever live will also face death on a predestined day. Despite this fact, people tend to see death as an unlikely incident.

Think of a baby who has just opened its eyes to the world and a man who is about to breathe his last. Both had no influence on their individual birth or death whatsoever. Only Allah possesses the power to inspire the breath of life or to take it away.

Brigitte Bardot

Marlon Brando

Katharine Hepburn

Fred Astaire

Charlie Chapline

Jane Russel

Kirk Douglas

Audrey Hepburn

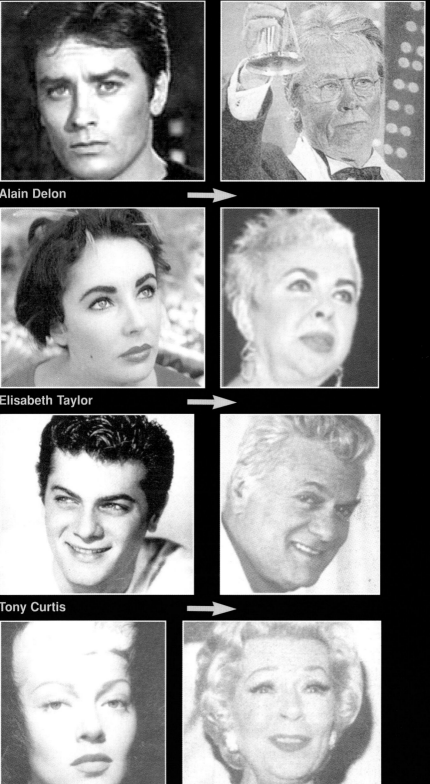

Alain Delon

Elisabeth Taylor

Tony Curtis

Lana Turner

Rita Hayworth

Frank Sinatra

All human beings will live until a certain day and then die; Allah in the Qur'an gives an account of the attitude commonly shown towards death in the following verse:

Say: "The death from which you flee will truly overtake you: then you will be sent back to the Knower of things secret and open: and He will tell you (the truth of) the things that you did!" (Surat al-Jumu'ah: 8)

The majority of people avoid thinking about death. In the rapid flow of daily events, a person usually occupies himself with totally different subjects: what college to enrol in, which company to work for, what colour of clothing to wear next morning, what to cook for supper; these are the kinds of major issues that we usually consider. Life is perceived as a routine process of such minor matters. Attempts to talk about death are always interrupted by those who do not feel comfortable hearing about it. Assuming death will come only when one grows older, one does not want to concern himself with such an unpleasant subject. Yet it should be kept in mind that living for even one further hour is never guaranteed. Everyday, man witnesses the deaths of people around him but thinks little about the day when others will witness his own death. He never supposes that such an end is awaiting him!

Nevertheless, when death comes to man, all the "realities" of life suddenly vanish. No reminder of the "good old days" endures in this world. Think of everything that you are able to do right now: you can blink your eyes, move your body, speak, laugh; all these are functions of your body. Now think about the state and shape your body will assume after your death.

From the moment you breathe for the last time, you will become nothing but a "heap of flesh". Your body, silent and motionless, will be carried to the morgue. There, it will be washed for the last time. Wrapped in a shroud, your corpse will be carried in a coffin to the graveyard. Once your remains are in the grave, soil will cover you. This is the end of your story. From now on, you are simply one of the names represented in the graveyard by a marble stone.

During the first months or years, your grave will be visited frequently.

As time passes, fewer people will come. Decades later, there will be no-one.

Meanwhile, your immediate family members will experience a different aspect of your death. At home, your room and bed will be empty. After the funeral, little of what belongs to you will be kept at home: most of your clothes, shoes, etc, will be given to those who need them. Your file at the public registration office will be deleted or archived. During the first years, some will mourn for you. Yet, time will work against the memories you left behind. Four or five decades later, there will remain only a few who remember you. Before long, new generations will come and none of your generation will exist any longer on earth. Whether you are remembered or not will be worthless to you.

While all this is taking place in the world, the corpse under the soil will go through a rapid process of decay. Soon after you are placed in the grave, the bacteria and insects proliferating in the corpse due to the absence of oxygen will start to function. The gasses released from these organisms will inflate the body, starting from the abdomen, altering its shape and appearance. Bloody froth will pop out the mouth and nose due to the pressure of gasses on the diaphragm. As corruption proceeds, body hair, nails, soles, and palms will fall off. Accompanying this outer alteration in the body, internal organs such as lungs, heart and liver will also decay. In the meantime, the most horrible scene takes place in the abdomen, where the skin can no longer bear the pressure of gasses and suddenly bursts, spreading an unendurably disgusting smell. Starting from the skull, muscles will detach from their particular places. Skin and soft tissues will completely disintegrate. The brain will decay and start looking like clay. This process will go on until the whole body is reduced to a skeleton.

There is no chance of going back to the old life again. Gathering around the supper table with family members, socialising or to having an honourable job will never again be possible.

In short, the "heap of flesh and bones" to which we assign an identity faces a quite nasty end. On the other hand, you – or rather, your soul – will leave this body as soon as you breathe your last. The remainder of you

– your body – will become part of the soil.

Yes, but what is the reason for all these things happening?

If Allah willed, the body would never have decayed in such a way. That it does so actually carries a very important inner message in itself.

The tremendous end awaiting man should make him acknowledge that he is not a body himself, but a soul "encased" within a body. In other words, man has to acknowledge that he has an existence beyond his body. Furthermore, man should understand the death of his body which he tries to possess as if he is to remain eternally in this temporal world. However this body, which he deems so important, will decay and become worm-eaten one day and finally be reduced to a skeleton. That day might be very soon.

Despite all these facts, man's mental process is inclined to disregard what he does not like or want. He is even inclined to deny the existence of things he avoids confronting. This tendency seems to be most apparent when death is the issue. Only a funeral or the sudden death of an immediate family member brings this reality to mind. Almost everybody sees death far from himself. The assumption is that those who die while sleeping or in an accident are different people and what they face will never befall us! Everybody thinks it is too early to die and that there are always years ahead to live.

Yet most probably, people who die on the way to school or hurrying to attend a business meeting shared the same thought. They probably never thought that the next day's newspapers would publish news of their deaths. It is entirely possible that, as you read these lines, you still do not expect to die soon after you have finished them or even entertain the possibility that it might happen. Probably you feel that it is too early to die because there are many things to accomplish. However, this is just an avoidance of death and these are only vain endeavours to escape it:

Say: "Running away will not profit you if you are running away from death or slaughter; and even if (you do escape), no more than a brief (respite) will you be allowed to enjoy!"(Surat al-Ahzab: 16)

Man who is created alone should be aware that he will also die alone.

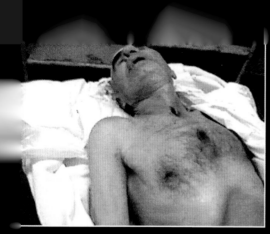

Just after death

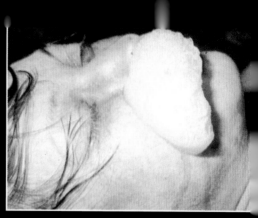

Bloody froth coming out of mouth and nos

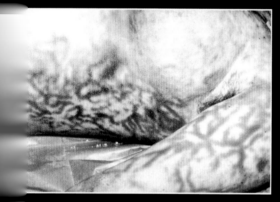

Before disintegration begins in the corpse

Eyes turning purple after death

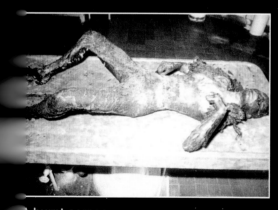

A burnt corpse

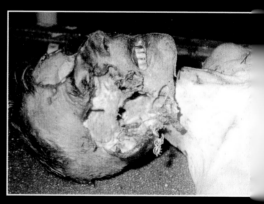

A corpse consumed by worms in a grave

Wherever you are, death will find you out,
even if you are in towers built up strong and high!

Yet during his life, he lives almost addicted to possessions. His sole purpose in life becomes to possess more. Yet, no-one can take his goods with him to the grave. The body is buried wrapped in a shroud made from the cheapest of fabrics. The body comes into this world alone and departs from it in the same way. The only asset one can take with him when one dies is one's belief or disbelief.

> *It is Allah Who created you in a state of (helpless) weakness, then gave (you) strength after weakness, then, after strength, gave (you) weakness and a hoary head: He creates as He wills, and it is He who has all knowledge and power. (Surat ar-Rum: 54)*

The Lure of Worldly Goods

Throughout life, we have particular goals to achieve: wealth, possessions, and better status, and a spouse and children. These are among the common goals shared by almost everyone. All planning and effort are designed to meet these goals. In spite of the sole incontrovertible fact that everything is inclined to age and extinction, people cannot keep themselves from becoming deeply attached to things. One day a brand-new car becomes old-fashioned; due to natural causes, rich farmland becomes barren; a beautiful person loses all her looks when she ages. Above all, every human being on earth dies, leaving everything he owned behind. Yet despite all these irrefutable facts, man shows an unfathomable devotion to possessions.

Those who spend their lives devoted blindly to worldly goods, will realise that they consumed all their lives chasing illusions. They will realise their ridiculous situation after they die. Only then will the ultimate purpose of life, to be a sincere servant of Allah, be clear to them.

Allah in the Qur'an gives a considerable account of this "deep attachment" in the following verse:

> Fair in the eyes of men is the love of things they covet: women and sons; heaped-up hoards of gold and silver; horses branded (for blood and excellence); and (wealth of) cattle and well-tilled land. Such are the possessions of this world's life; but in nearness to Allah is the best of the goals (to return to). (Surah Ali-'Imran: 14)

All the matters of this world – wealth, spouses, children and commerce – keep many a person busy in this life. However, if they could acknowledge the power and greatness of Allah, they would know that all the things granted to man are merely means of obtaining His good pleasure. This way, they would also comprehend that the main aim of man is to be His servant. Yet, those who do not have true faith and trust in Allah have blurred vision and a poor understanding of their existence due to their worldly ambitions. They expect great things from this flawed life.

It is surprising that man forgets all about the Hereafter, which is a perfect and infinitely superior residence for him, and is satisfied with this world. If someone does not have complete faith, even the existence of a slight "probability" of the Hereafter should make him, at least, assume a more cautious attitude.

Believers, on the other hand, are fully aware that this is, by no means, a "probability" but a reality. That is why their lives serve the purpose of eradicating the slightest possibility of being sent to hell; their efforts are entirely designed to attain paradise. They know clearly that the disappointment felt in the Hereafter after a life spent on vain desires will be bitter. They are well aware that accumulated wealth, such as an overflowing bank account, luxury cars or mansions, will not be accepted as a ransom from eternal punishment. Furthermore, neither family nor one's dearest friends will be present to save one from eternal grief. On the contrary, every soul will try to save itself. Yet despite all this, most people assume that this life does not continue on to the hereafter, and greedily embrace this world. Allah states this in the verse below:

> Mutual rivalry for piling up (the good things of this world) diverts you (from the more serious things), until you visit the graves. (Surat at-Takathur: 1-2)

Attraction towards worldly possessions is, no doubt, the secret of the test. Allah creates all things that He bestows upon man with great sophistication, yet they are also of short duration. This is only to make people think and compare the things given to them in this world with the Hereafter. This is the "secret" of which we are talking. Life in the world is indeed magnificent; it is quite colourful and attractive revealing the glory of Allah's creation. To lead a good life and take pleasure in it is, no doubt, something desirable and man, surely, prays to Allah to lead such a life. Yet this can never be the ultimate purpose, since such a goal in life is not more important than attaining the good pleasure of Allah and paradise. Therefore, man should never forget his main purpose, while enjoying the benefit of these favours. Allah warns man about this issue in the verse below:

> The (material) things which you are given are but the conveniences of this life and the glitter thereof; but that which is with Allah is better and more enduring: will you not then be wise? (Surat al-Qasas: 60)

This great fondness for worldly things is one of the reasons why man forgets the Hereafter. There is another point to remember: man never finds true happiness in any of the worldly things he greedily embraces or in any provision that he toils to possess. That is because keen desires are hard to satisfy. No matter how much it may possess, the desires of the ego never end. Typically, it always seeks for more and for better. This is why the human being cannot find peace or satisfaction in the world.

Does Real Wealth Exist in this World?

A majority of people assume they can turn their life into a perfect one once they determine to do so. Furthermore, they simply assume that achieving a high quality of life is possible through having more money, better living standards, a happy family, and an admirable status in society. Yet, those people who devote all their time to securing such things are clearly admitting to an error. First, they only struggle to attain peace and happiness in this world and forget all about the Hereafter. Despite the fact that their main purpose is to be servants of Allah in this world and to be grateful for what He gives, they spend life fulfilling their own vain desires.

Allah informs man about the insignificance and deceptive allure of the world in the Qur'an:

> Know you (all), that the life of this world is but play and amusement, pomp and mutual boasting and multiplying (in rivalry) among yourselves, riches and children. Here is a similitude: how rain and the growth which it brings

forth delight (the hearts of) the tillers; soon it withers; you will see it grow yellow; then it becomes dry and crumbles away. But in the Hereafter is a penalty severe (for the devotees of wrong). And forgiveness from Allah and (His) good pleasure (for the devotees of Allah). And what is the life of this world, but goods and chattels of deception? (Surat al-Hadid: 20)

Not believing in the Hereafter or seeing it as a remote possibility is the many people's fundamental mistake. They believe that they will never lose their wealth. Pride makes them avoid submission to Allah and turn their faces against His promise. The ends of such people are related as follows:

Those who rest not their hope on their meeting with Us, but are pleased and satisfied with the life of the present, and those who heed not Our signs: Their abode is hell, because of the (evil) they earned. (Surah Yunus: 7-8)

History has witnessed many such people. Kings, emperors, and pharaohs thought they could secure immortality through their fabulous wealth; the thought that there is something more valuable than wealth and power may never even have occurred to them. This flawed mentality mis-led their peoples, who were greatly impressed by their wealth and power. However, all these disbelievers faced a terrible end. In the Qur'an, Allah informs us about them:

Do they think that because We have granted them abundance of wealth and sons, We would hasten them on in every good? Nay, they do not understand. (Surat al-Muminun: 55- 56)

Let not their wealth nor their (following in) sons dazzle you: in reality Allah's plan is to punish them with these things in this life, and that their souls may perish in their (very) denial of Allah. (Surat at-Tawbah: 55)

These people actually disregard a crucial point. All wealth and every-thing deemed important, belong to Allah. Allah, the actual Owner of wealth, allocates His endless possessions among those whom He wills. In return, man is expected to show his gratefulness to Allah and be a loyal servant to Him. It should be remembered that nobody can limit one's pos-sessions once Allah bestows them. Likewise, once somebody is deprived of affluence, nobody except Allah has the power to sustain him. In this way, Allah puts His people to test. However, those who forget their Creator and the day of judgement pay no heed to this:

A drawing of a Mayan monument in Honduras. (Bottom) The current state of the same monument, once the symbol of a magnificent civilisation. The comparison reveals a striking fact: no magnificence is immune to destruction in this world.

These are some of the stories of communities that We relate to you: of them, some are standing, and some have been mown down (by the sickle of time).

(Surah Hud: 100)

Only a theatre survives from the glorious ancient Roman metropolis, which is now replaced with a totally different look. (Right) The current situation of the same theatre. Today, there is no trace of anyone having lived there in glory.

Allah enlarges, or grants by (strict) measure, the sustenance (which He gives) to whomsoever He pleases. (The worldly) rejoice in the life of this world. But the life of this world is but little comfort in the Hereafter. (Surat ar-Ra'd: 26)

Are Wealth and Status in the World Important?

Most people believe that a perfectly peaceful life is attainable in this world. This mentality suggests that one can find true happiness and earn the respect of others by becoming wealthy. The same mentality believes that once this contentment is fulfilled, it will last until the end of the world. Yet, the truth is otherwise. Man can never achieve the life of his dreams by forgetting his Creator and the day of judgement. That is because by the time he realises one goal, he sets his mind on others. Not content with earning a lot, he goes into new businesses. He does not take any pleasure from his new flat once he sees his neighbour's more artfully decorated house, or else, because the fact that his house is decorated in last year's style, which is no longer in fashion, prompts him to redecorate it. Similarly, since fashions and tastes change dramatically, he dreams of a more sophisticated wardrobe because he is not satisfied with what he already has. The psychology of disbelievers is clearly explained in the following verse:

> Leave Me alone, (to deal) with the (creature) whom I created (bare and) alone! To whom I granted resources in abundance, sons dwelling in his presence to whom I made (life) smooth and comfortable! Yet is he greedy that I should add (yet more). (Surat al-Muddaththir: 11-15)

A person of sound mind and clear understanding should acknowledge that those who possess mansions with more rooms than inhabitants, luxury cars or fabulous wardrobes are only able to use a limited part of those possessions. If you had the biggest mansion in the world, would it be possible to enjoy the comfort of each room at the same time? Alternatively, if you had a wardrobe of highly fashionable clothes, how many of your suits could you wear in a day? The owner of a mansion with dozens of rooms, as an entity limited in terms of time and space can only stay in a single room at any one time. If you are offered all the delicious dishes of a famous cuisine, your stomach would take no more than a few of them; if you attempt to bolt down more, the result will be torture rather than pleasure.

The list could be further extended, yet the most striking fact is that man is destined to a quite limited period of life in which he can enjoy the luxury his wealth brings. Man rapidly proceeds towards his end, yet he hardly acknowledges this during his life and assumes that his wealth will bring him eternal happiness, as the verse suggests:

> Thinking that his wealth would make him last forever! (Surat al-Humazah: 3)

Man is so blindly fascinated with the power of his wealth that when he faces the awful end on the day of judgement, he will still struggle to escape from punishment by giving away his wealth:

> Though they will be put in sight of each other, - the wrongdoer's desire will be: Would that he could redeem himself from the penalty of that day by (sacrificing) his children, wife and his brother, kindred who sheltered him, all that

is on earth so it could deliver him: by no means! For it would be the fire of hell! (Surat al-Ma'arij: 11-15)

Yet, some people are aware that wealth, prosperity and great fortune are under the control of Allah. Hence, they are well aware that rank and status are ridiculous. Only these people truly understand that these possessions will not save them in the hereafter. Therefore, they do not dare to chase after the valuables of this world. Showing arrogance is not a trait you can expect from such modest people. Never forgetting the existence of Almighty Allah makes them feel grateful for everything He gives them. In return for such conduct, Allah promises an honourable and comfortable life to them. The people who trust in Allah and make their servanthood to Allah the ultimate purpose of their lives are aware that they can only benefit from worldly goods for a limited period of time and that worldly goods are worthless next to the eternal abundance promised. Wealth never makes such people become deeply attached to this life. On the contrary, it makes them more grateful and closer to Allah. They deal justly with everyone and every issue, and try, with what Allah gives them, to attain His good pleasure. Rather than taking pleasure from wealth in this world, they aim to acquire the Qur'anic values expected from them, fully aware that real status and praise in the presence of Allah matter. The prophet Sulayman set an example to all people as an honourable believer who showed such traits in his life. Possessing a great wealth and sovereignty, Sulayman clearly stated why he pursued this wealth:

> Truly do I love the love of good, with a view to the glory of my Lord. (Surah Sad: 32)

Failure to acknowledge why worldly goods are created in this world leads people to forget that they will only be able to use these possessions for a period of 60-70 years, if they are destined to live that long, and then leave their mansions, cars and children behind. They do not think that they will be buried alone in their graves. All through their lives they long for the affluence they will never be able to enjoy.

Yet, those who consider wealth a saviour and neglect the existence of their Creator suffer bitter grief both in this world and the hereafter:

Those who reject faith, neither their possessions nor their (numerous) progeny will avail them aught against Allah: They are themselves but fuel for hell. (Surah Ali-'Imran: 10)

The Qur'an heralds the end of those who demonstrate insatiable greed for possessions:

Who heaps up wealth and lay it by,
Thinking that his wealth would make him last forever!
By no means! He will definitely be thrown into That which breaks to pieces,
And what will explain to you That which breaks to pieces?
(It is) hell of (the wrath of) Allah kindled (to a blaze),
Which mounts (right) to the hearts.
It shall be made into a vault over them,
In columns outstretched. (Surat al-Humazah: 2-9)

True wealth belongs to those believers who never show an inner interest in possessions in this world and truly believe that only Allah gives everything to man. These are actually the really wealthy people in this world; they do not limit their lives to a mere 50-60 years. Believers engage in the best trade by obtaining paradise in exchange for this life. They prefer permanent instead of temporary wealth. Allah informs us about this in the following verse:

Allah has purchased from the believers their persons and their goods; for theirs (in return) is the Garden (of Paradise): they fight in His cause, and slay and are slain: a promise binding on Him in truth, through the Tawrah, the Gospel, and the Qur'an: and who is more faithful to his covenant than Allah? Then rejoice in the bargain which you have concluded: that is the achievement supreme. (Surat at-Tawbah: 111)

Disregarding these facts, those who "cling to" this world will soon understand clearly who is on the path of right action.

Marriage

Marriage is considered an important turning point in one's life. Every young girl or boy looks forward to meeting the person of her or his dreams. A good mate is a major goal in life and young people are almost "indoctrinated" with the importance of finding one. However, relations between man and woman are fundamentally based on unsound grounds in ignorant societies, namely societies in which people do not accept the Qur'anic way of life: "friendships" are solely romantic relationships in which both sexes seek emotional satisfaction. Yet, marriages are usually based on mutual material benefits. Many women try to find a "prosperous man" in expectation of a high standard of living. For such a purpose, a young girl may easily accept to be the life-long spouse of someone for whom she has no affection. On the other hand, what a man seeks in a woman is very often "good looks".

Yet the rationale behind the viewpoint of an ignorant society neglects a crucial fact: all these materialistic values are eventually doomed to perish; Allah can take back the fortune of a man in a moment. Similarly, it takes but a few seconds to lose good looks; as city dwellers, for instance, our daily commuting to and from work can at any time be thwarted by an accident that may leave hideous and permanent scars on the face. Time, meanwhile, deals irrecoverable damage to our health, strength and beauty. Under such unpredictable conditions, what consequences are there in a system based on purely materialistic values? For instance, think of a man who only marries a woman because he is impressed by her good looks. What would he think if her face is badly injured in an accident? Would he leave her when wrinkles start to appear on her face? The answers no doubt reveal the unreasonable basis of materialistic thinking.

A marriage becomes precious when it is intended purely to obtain the good pleasure of Allah. Otherwise, it becomes a burden both in this world and the next. If not in this world, man will ultimately understand in the hereafter that this is an improper way for the human soul. Yet, this will be too late; on the day of judgement, he would hold his wife, to whom he felt so close in this world, a ransom for his own salvation. The terror of that day will render all relations in this world meaningless. Allah gives a detailed account of the relationships between immediate family members on the day of judgement in the following verse:

> Though they will be put in sight of each other, the wrongdoer's desire will be: would that he could redeem himself from the penalty of that Day by (sacrificing) his children, wife and his brother, kindred who sheltered him... (Surat al-Ma'arij: 11-13)

It is evident from the verses that people will no longer attach any importance to women, friends, brothers or sisters on the day of judgement. In their desperate efforts to be saved, everybody will be willing to pay their immediate family or relatives as a ransom for their own personal salvation. Furthermore, these people will curse each other since they never warned each other against such a terrible end. In the Qur'an, the case of Abu Lahab who deserved eternal punishment in hell and his wife is recounted:

> The power of Abu Lahab will perish, and he will perish. His wealth and gains will not exempt him. He will be plunged in flaming fire, and his wife, the wood-carrier, will have upon her neck a halter of palm-fibre. (Surat al-Masad: 1-5)

The type of marriage acceptable in the presence of Allah is, however, based on totally different criteria. Contrary to the marriages common in an ignorant society, where people are heedless about earning the good pleasure of Allah, the criteria is not money, fame or beauty but a marriage intended to gain His good pleasure. For believers, the only criterion is taqwa, in other words, 'the avoidance of all that is prohibited, the fulfilment of all that is commanded, and the fear of Allah. Consequently, a believer can only marry someone who displays a deep loyalty to Allah. People find peace and happiness in this marriage. The relevant verse follows:

> And among His Signs is this, that He created for you mates from among yourselves, that you may dwell in tranquillity with them, and He has put love and mercy between your (hearts): verily in that are Signs for those who reflect. (Surat ar-Rum: 21)

Taqwa being the sole bond, believers will surely meet a pleasant life in the Hereafter. As they remind each other righteousness and guide one another to the paradise all through their lives, they will also remain close friends for all eternity. Their relations are described as follows:

> The believers, men and women, are protectors one of another: they enjoin what is just, and forbid what is evil: they observe regular prayers, practice regular charity, and obey Allah and His messenger. On them will Allah pour His mercy: for Allah is exalted in power, Wise. (Surat at-Tawbah: 71)

Children

A major ambition of mankind is to leave behind sons who will carry the family name into the future. However, if not intended seeking the good pleasure of Allah, this ambition well may be a factor taking man from the path of Allah. A person is tested in his children; in this sense, what is expected from him is to treat them in a way that will gain the good pleasure of Allah.

> Your wealth and your children are only a trial, whereas Allah! With Him is an immense reward. (Surat at-Taghabun: 15)

In the verse, the use of the word 'trial' is of great significance. For many people, having children is one of the most important goals in life. Yet in the Qur'anic sense, a believer only wants children in order to gain the good pleasure of Allah. Otherwise, just for the sake of satisfying one's own desire for a child, having a baby would only mean ascribing partners to Allah. The example of those who forget their real purpose and make their children the "ultimate goal in life" is given in the Qur'an:

> He it is Who did create you from a single soul, and therefrom did make his mate that he might take rest in her. And when he covered her she bore a light burden, and she passed (unnoticed) with it, but when it became heavy they cried to Allah, their Lord, saying: "If you give to us a goodly child, we vow we shall be of the thankful." When He gave to them a goodly child, they ascribed to Him partners in respect of that which He had given them. High is He exalted above all that they associate (with Him). Do they indeed ascribe to Him as partners things that can create nothing, but are themselves created? (Surat al-A'raf: 189-191)

Believers ask for children from Allah only for His good pleasure. When asking for children, the prophets cited in the Qur'an only intended to attain the good pleasure of Allah. An example is the wife of 'Imran:

> When the wife of 'Imran said: "My Lord! Surely I vow to You what is in my womb, to be devoted (to Your service); accept therefore from me, surely You are the Hearing, the Knowing." (Surat Ali-'Imran 35)

The prayer of the prophet Ibrahim, also sets an example to all believers:

Our Lord! Make of us Muslims, bowing to Your (Will), and of our progeny a people Muslim, bowing to Your (will); and show us our place for the celebration of (due) rites; and turn unto us (in Mercy); for You are the Oft-Returning, Most Merciful. (Surat al-Baqarah: 128)

In the expression of the verse, having children, if intended to seek Allah's favour, is a way of worshipping Allah. However, when the real intention is something other than attaining the blessing of Allah, then a person may suffer grave consequences both in this world and the next. Believers acknowledge their children as individuals entrusted to them by Allah. Therefore, they do not take a personal pride in their children's appearance, success or intelligence, knowing that Allah granted those traits to that child. Such pride is simply an act of going astray.

Such an approach has detrimental consequences in the hereafter. On the day of judgement, one would be more than willing to pay one's sons, spouse and other immediate family members as ransom for eternal salvation. One's desire to avoid the awful punishment makes one immediately forsake beloved ones. Yet on the day of judgement there will be no hope of escaping eternal punishment by such an act.

For the people of an ignorant society, children become the source of many problems not only in the hereafter but also in this world. From birth onwards, rearing a child entails burdensome responsibilities for parents. It is an especially difficult experience for the pregnant mother. First, the day she receives the news of a baby, she has to change her life-style entirely. She has to reorder her priorities. In this respect the needs of the baby in her womb always come first; her eating habits, the way she sleeps, in brief, her whole personal life changes entirely. Towards the end of the period of pregnancy, doing daily work and most simple bodily movements become impossible for the mother. Yet, the major difficulties start after birth. The mother spends all her time taking care of the baby. The baby usually leaves its mother very little time for her personal needs and tasks. Therefore, the mother looks forward to the time when her baby grows old enough to take care of its own needs. In the meantime, the mother does not recognise how quickly the years pass. If done for the good pleasure of

Allah, such a long time can be considered as a way of worship. Yet for the members of an ignorant society, these years are nothing more than pointless trouble.

Parents in an ignorant society usually feel disappointment when they raise their family. Raised as a member of an ignorant society, the child generally develops a self-centred personality. Under the misguidance of selfish drives and motives, he shows interest in the needs of his parents only if it serves him to do so. His parents, now old and experiencing age-related problems, only understand this fact late in life. However in the early years of parenthood, they imagine that when their children grow up they would be major supports in times of unexpected trouble, but contrary to this expectation, they may even find themselves in rest-homes.

Allah in the Qur'an presents man with a framework, according to which believers must conduct themselves responsibly towards their parents. Allah requires respect and mercy towards parents, especially those in old age:

> Your Lord has decreed that you worship none but Him, and that you be kind to parents. Whether one or both of them attain old age in your lifetime, say not to them a word of contempt, nor repel them, but address them in terms of honour. And, out of kindness, lower to them the wing of humility, and say: "My Lord! Bestow on them your mercy even as they cherished me in childhood." (Surat al-Isra: 23-24)

As we understand from the verses, rearing a child in the light of Qur'anic values is something honourable for believers to do. Yet, if unbelieving people who force the children to adopt the mentality of an ignorant society rear them, then this is a vain effort both in this world and the next. Furthermore, believers still attain the good pleasure of Allah even if the child does not adopt the Qur'anic teaching he is given. Parents are only held responsible to give the Qur'anic teaching to their children and then put their trust in Allah. Besides Allah, people have no other protector or helper.

Those who seek worldly benefits from their children will receive no help from them either in this world or in the next.

> When the Deafening Blast comes, the Day a man will flee from his brother and his mother and his father, and his wife and his children: on that Day every man among them will have concerns enough of his own. (Surah 'Abasa: 33-37)

As stated earlier, man is only created to serve his Creator. Everything surrounding him, all his life only exists to test him. After death, a person will only be judged according to his deeds. In return for his deeds, he will be rewarded with paradise or punished in hell. In brief, wealth, beauty or sons are not worthwhile, but taqwa, the "Fear of Allah" is worthwhile.

It is neither your wealth nor your sons that will bring you nearer to Us in degree: but only those who believe and work right actions, these are the ones for whom there is a multiplied reward for their deeds, while secure they (reside) in the dwellings on high! (Surah Saba: 37)

Those who reject faith, neither their possessions nor their (numerous) progeny will avail them aught against Allah: they will be companions of hell, dwelling therein (forever). (Surah Ali-'Imran: 116)

Of no profit whatever to them, against Allah, will be their riches or their sons: they will be companions of hell, to dwell therein (for aye)! (Surat al-Mujadilah: 17)

Natural Hazards and Disasters

T he world is anything but serene and still. We are all vulnerable to natural threats, both internal and external. Meteor showers, asteroids are only a few of the factors likely to pose threats to the world from space. As for the seemingly solid earth, the planet's interior has an inner core of molten elements. It surely would not be an exaggeration to call this part of the earth, which remains invisible to our eyes, "a flaming core". There also exists an atmosphere surrounding the earth, which is a "shield" against external threats. Yet, no part of the earth is immune against the effects of atmospheric forces like thunderstorms, storms, or hurricanes.

Natural hazards may strike at any time. They can cause considerable loss of life and property. Generally referred to as "natural" disasters, earthquakes, lightning, flash floods, global wildfires, acid rain, and tidal waves have different intensities and effects. What is common to all these disasters is that in just moments they can reduce a city, with all its inhabitants, to ruin. What is most important, no human being has the power to combat or prevent any of these hazards.

Heavy destruction is the legacy of catastrophes all over the planet. Yet, a disaster always affects only a particular region of the earth, thanks to nature's delicate balance which is a creation of Allah. A significant protection exists on earth for all living things as well as for human beings. The possibility of a devastating natural disaster always lurks in spite of this protection. Allah creates these disasters to show us how insecure our habitation can sometimes be. These outbursts of nature are reminders to all mankind that we have no control whatsoever over the planet. Likewise, each disaster serves the purpose of reminding us of our inherent weakness. These are surely warnings to those that can contemplate the significance of such events and draw lessons from the experience of others.

What other lessons should man learn from natural disasters?

The world is specially created for man. The reason why man is created is evident as the verse suggests:

> "He it is who created the heavens and the earth in six Days, and His Throne was over the waters, that He might try you, which of you is best in conduct." (Surah Hud: 7)

The "setting" for this "test" is quite elaborate, however, and each event is a component of this sophisticated setting. Furthermore, none of these natural phenomena occur randomly; all have a scientific explanation. For instance, the earth's gravitational force explains why we do not drift off into space; rain falls when water vapour reaches a certain level of saturation. The same kind of causation is also valid for death, accidents or disease. Numerous causes can be cited for why a man dies, becomes sick, or has an accident. Yet, what really matters is not the number of these reasons but the "reliability" of the system these causes and their consequences rest upon. One particular aspect of this system is important; each incident proceeds in a way such that the human mind can entirely understand it. Allah warns man by means of natural disasters. An earthquake, for instance, kills thousands of women, children and young people and leaves many more injured. Those who are heedless of the warnings of Allah are prone to explain such incidents as "natural" phenomena and little understand that Allah creates these for specific purposes. Let us think for a moment: what would happen if only those who are guilty before Allah died in an earthquake? In such a case, the appropriate basis for the "test" of humankind would not be established. That is why Allah creates each phenomenon in a "natural" setting. Only those who are aware of the existence of Allah and have a deep comprehension of His creation understand the divine rationale behind this "natural" appearance.

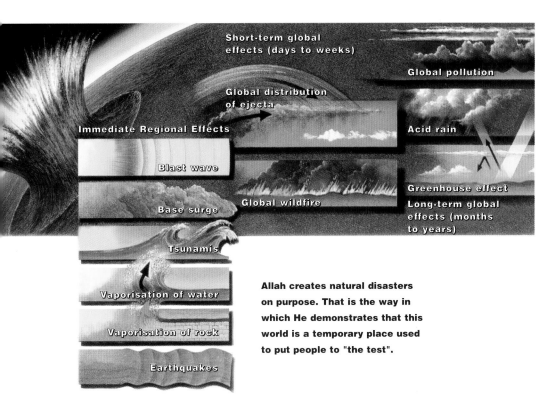

Short-term global effects (days to weeks)

Global pollution

Global distribution of ejecta

Immediate Regional Effects

Acid rain

Blast wave

Base surge

Global wildfire

Greenhouse effect

Long-term global effects (months to years)

Tsunamis

Vaporisation of water

Vaporisation of rock

Earthquakes

Allah creates natural disasters on purpose. That is the way in which He demonstrates that this world is a temporary place used to put people to "the test".

In the verse, "Every soul shall taste death: and We test you by evil and by good by way of trial. To Us must you return," (Surat al-Anbiya: 35), Allah states that He tests man through good as well as bad events.

That many people are affected by a disaster is the riddle of this test. One should always keep in mind that Allah is the All-Knowing Judge and "the Decision between them at judgement will be in perfect justice." (Surat az-Zumar: 75).

All events happening to a person in this life are a part of the test. Those who are truly believers comprehend the essence of this riddle. Whenever a misfortune befalls them, they turn to Allah alone and repent. They are servants of Allah and are aware of the promise of Allah:

> Be sure We shall test you with something of fear and hunger, some loss in goods and lives and the fruits (of your toil), but give glad tidings to those who patiently persevere, who say, when afflicted with calamity: "To Allah we belong, and to Him is our return". They are those on whom (descend) blessings from Allah, and mercy, and they are the ones that receive guidance. (Surat al-Baqarah: 155- 157)

As is stated in the verse, all people, believers and disbelievers, are tested in many ways: sometimes by natural disaster, at other times by something happening in our daily lives, a disease or an accident that befalls us. Such misfortunes strike individuals as well as societies and cause material loss along with spiritual suffering. A wealthy man may become bankrupt, a girl with good looks may receive a severe injury on the face, or a city may be reduced to rubble by an earthquake. These incidents are all clear demonstrations of how, at any moment, events can alter our lives.

People should be able to draw lessons from these events. No doubt, Allah does not create anything without a purpose; each disaster is a reminder for human beings whose purpose is to save humans from the perversity they are in. In the Qur'an, Allah says that without His leave, nothing can occur on earth:

> No kind of calamity can occur, except by the leave of Allah: and if anyone believes in Allah, (Allah) guides his heart (aright): for Allah knows all things. (Surat at-Taghabun: 11)
>
> Nor can a soul die except by Allah's leave, the term being fixed as by writing. If any desires a reward in this life, We shall give it to him; and if any desires a reward in the hereafter, We shall give it to him. And swiftly shall We reward those that (serve Us with) gratitude. (Surah Ali-'Imran: 145)

Another lesson one draws from disasters is that man, assuming himself to be mighty on earth, realises that he is simply weak and actually does not have the strength to cope with disasters, which happen in a moment by the will of Allah. Man can provide no help either to himself or to anyone else. Surely Allah is Omnipotent. This is stated in the following verse:

> If Allah touch you with affliction, none can remove it but He; if He touch you with happiness, He has power over all things. (Surat al-An'am: 17)

In this chapter, a comprehensive account of types of disasters affecting the earth will be given. The purpose is to remind people that this world is not a place for which to feel blind affection. These incidents indicate how desperately we need Allah's guidance and help. This desperation is a clear statement that people are impotent before Allah. As is said in the verse; "and nor have you, besides Allah, any protector or helper." (Surat al-'Ankabut: 22)

Earthquakes

Earthquakes are the most devastating natural forces on earth. The worst loss of life occurs during earthquakes. Research reveals that every two minutes somewhere the surface of the earth cracks. According to statistics, the earth shakes millions of times a year. On average, the intensity of three hundred thousand of these earthquakes is minor; they are imperceptible tremors and cause no destruction at all. Twenty of them, on the other hand, are powerful earthquakes which convulse the land. Yet since they often do not hit densely populated areas, they kill few people, if any, and cause little economic loss. Only five of these earthquakes reduce buildings to heaps of rubble.

This information shows that people do not frequently encounter earthquakes. No doubt, this is Allah's special protection against disasters for humankind.

In our day, only a city or a province becomes subject to damaging earthquakes. Yet, by the will of Allah, an earthquake affecting the whole planet could happen at any time. This type of shaking of the ground could end life on earth. The structure of the earth is quite vulnerable to quakes; a sudden movement or rupture of large masses of rock within the earth's crust or upper mantle would make catastrophe inescapable.

An earthquake has no relation with the type of soil that amplifies the effects of seismic waves travelling through it. An earthquake may still occur even when the natural conditions for an earthquake do not exist. By the will of Allah, an earthquake may happen at any time. Yet, Allah specially creates insecurity and instability in some parts of the land. This is to remind people that, at any time, an unexpected incident may place their lives in jeopardy. In the Qur'an, Allah warns people against a possible calamity:

> Do those who plot evil actions feel secure that Allah will not cause the earth to swallow them up or that a punishment will not come upon them from where they least expect? Or that He will not seize them on their travels, something they are powerless to prevent? Or that He will not seize them little by little? For your Lord is All-Compassionate, Most Merciful. (Surat an-Nahl: 45-47)

These earthquakes shaking the earth for only seconds can last for hours, even days. While recovering from a devastating disaster, people can suffer another. This is surely easy for Allah. However, by His mercy, Allah protects man and with such disasters reminds him, now and then, that he has no control whatsoever over his life.

At this point, it could be beneficial to remember a major earthquake, which took place in the 20th century.

Technology Defeated: Kobe

Today's advanced level of science and technology inspires man with the feeling that he has control over nature. Yet, those who are overwhelmed by such a notion may soon feel disappointment. Technology is a tool provided by Allah for the service of man and is entirely under His control. Various events show that even the most advanced technology is impotent to rule nature.

For instance, despite the "earthquake-resistant technology" developed by Japanese scientists, Kobe fell victim to widespread subsidence caused by twenty seconds of intense shock waves during the 1995 quake. The world's most earthquake-resistant structures built to withstand an intense jolt simply collapsed during a momentary 6.9 magnitude quake. During the previous three decades, the Japanese government had invested 40 trillion dollars in academic research to develop warning systems for earthquakes. Yet, these efforts yielded no conclusive results at all. As the millennium draws to a close, scientists are still unable to devise systems to issue warnings that could reduce the destructive effects of dangerous seismic events. Kobe was a recent example, among many others, demonstrating how vulnerable to unexpected patterns of seismic hits a modern industrialised city is.

The public was reassured that modern technology developed to predict major earthquakes would save them from complete destruction. Yet, after the disaster which reduced Kobe to heaps of rubble, it became apparent that no technology had been available to alert people to the danger. It also became apparent that the so-called "quake-resistant structures" had no resistance at all to the earthquake whose epicentre was 15 miles southwest of downtown Kobe.

Kobe, Japan's second most densely populated industrialised city and most important port after Tokyo. At 5:46 am on the 17th January 1995, twenty seconds of intense shock waves caused appalling damage. Only twenty seconds and everything people had toiled their whole lives to possess was destroyed.

The region affected by the earthquake included the populous cities of Kobe and Osaka. That is why appalling damage occurred, leaving 5,200 people dead and another 300,000 injured. The total damage was put at 200 billion dollars.[3]

There are certainly lessons to be drawn from such a disaster. City-dwellers, used to leading comfortable lives, were suddenly confronted with many hardships after the disaster. In a state of shock, they were unable to figure out what to do with their lives,- let alone make plans for the future.

Typhoons, Hurricanes, Tornadoes...

Typhoons, hurricanes, and tornadoes are natural disasters that people frequently experience. These disasters and their aftermaths claim thousands of lives every year. These are very strong winds, which can cause great damage to cities, killing and injuring residents, hurling thousands of trees, huts, telephone poles, cars, and even buildings miles away.

Great typhoons in particular can cause giant sea waves to raise suddenly from the seabed. In this phenomenon, powerful storms send waves speeding at hundreds of miles per hour across the ocean against seacoasts. In such cases, water rises onto the land and heavy rains cause serious floods in delta regions.

The transformation of winds that are generally experienced as mild breezes into powerful storms capable of moving buildings no doubt forces us to look for the great power making such events happen. The same rationale discussed in the section on earthquakes is also true for typhoons, hurricanes and tornadoes: if Allah willed it so, man would very frequently be confronted by such natural disasters. While recovering from disaster, human beings could suffer another. In the Qur'an, Allah reminds man that winds are under His control:

> Do you feel secure against Him Who is in heaven causing the earth to swallow you up when suddenly it rocks from side to side? Or do you feel secure against Him Who is in heaven releasing against you a sudden squall of stones, so that you will know how true My warning was? Those before them also denied but then how great was My denial! (Surat al-Mulk: 16-18)

However, Allah protects man against hazards. He only occasionally sends against them violent storms. This is surely to give man a warning. The intention is to remind people that their ultimate purpose in life is to be servants of Allah, that they are but impotent against Allah's might and that they will be judged on the day of judgement.

Volcanoes

As well as the vibration or shaking of the ground caused by sudden movement or rupture of large masses of rock within the earth's crust or upper mantle, volcanic eruptions are another spectacular form of natural disaster. There are about 1,500 active volcanoes around the world today; 550[4] of them exist on land while the remainder are under the oceans. These volcanoes can erupt at any time in extremely destructive ways that no-one can anticipate in advance. When they erupt, they can kill the residents of nearby cities in addition to destroying crops and covering farmland with ash.

Some catastrophic eruptions that took place in this century as well as earlier in history made indelible impressions on the human mind. These eruptions wiped many cities off the map and killed numerous communities.

There are certainly lessons to be drawn from the volcanic eruptions witnessed in history. Mount Vesuvius in Italy, for instance, buried **Pompeii**, a city whose residents led a life of total debauchery, under a storm of hot lava. It is striking that 20,000 inhabitants of this prosperous city were asphyxiated mostly by the pyroclastic flows that swept through it on the 24th August 79 CE.

In our own day, however, the dormancy of volcanoes can often end abruptly and they can explode at unexpected times shooting steam and ash thousands of feet into the air. In the meantime, pyroclastic flows sweep through areas causing irrecoverable damage to whatever they encounter. Another adverse effect of eruptions is the harmful clouds of gases and ash carried by winds into populated areas. These terrifying winds, sometimes about 90 miles per hour, set everything on fire and engulf cities like sun-extinguishing canopies.

In February 1988, a hurricane caused extensive damage when it struck Florida. The hurricane demolished buildings and hurled automobiles onto buildings. (Next and below) Automobiles and households scattered by the hurricane.

A tornado big enough to sweep away homes and reduce a whole city to rubble.

In February 1988, after a hurricane's passing in Florida, a heap of powerboats.

One of history's worst disasters occurred in 1883 when Krakatau, in the East Indies, erupted explosively, generating a sound-wave heard 3,000 miles away and creating tsunamis up to 125 feet high. The waves razed 165 coastal villages and killed 36,000 people.[5]

Volcanoes are memorable not only for their tragically high death tolls but also because they erupt in extremely destructive ways that cannot be predicted. The eruption of Nevado Del Ruiz is an example. This was an eruption of minor intensity. In comparison, its intensity was only 3% of the eruption of Mount St Helens. After being dormant for 150 years, Nevado Del Ruiz erupted in 1985 melting the snow and ice on its summit. So devastating was the lahar, or river of mud, that flowed down the volcano's slopes and into the Lagunille River valley, that some 20,000 residents in Armero, Colombia perished, entombed in hot mud as they slept. This event was the worst volcanic disaster since Mount Pelee annihilated St Pierre in 1902. Mount Pelee claimed 30,000 lives when it sent a nuee ardente, or pyroclastic flow, into the town of St Pierre.[6]

Allah demonstrates how suddenly man can meet his death by means of such disasters and thereby calls on him to ponder the purpose of his exis-

(Left) A volcano erupting. (Below) The bus in the middle of the sea of lava reminds one of the Pompeii disaster.

Filling the entire horizon in June 1991, searing clouds of ash-laden gas – a lethal pyroclastic surge – spew from Mount Pinatubo in one of the 20th century's most violently explosive eruptions. (Below) Residents around Mount Pinatubo protect themselves with umbrellas against ash-rain.[7] (Left)

tence on earth. These incidents send a "warning". What is expected in return from man, who can conceive of his Almighty Creator, is not to indulge distractedly in the affairs of a short life of 50-60 years and neglect the eternal life, the hereafter. We should keep in mind that death will come upon all men one day and that everybody will be judged in the presence of Allah:

> One day the earth will be changed to a different earth, and so will be the heavens, and (men) will be marshalled forth, before Allah, the One, the Irresistable. (Surah Ibrahim: 48)

Tsunamis

Seismic sea waves or tidal waves are caused by a sudden uplift or subsidence of the sea floor or by volcanic eruptions. Some tsunamis can be as destructive as atom bombs.

Floods

Allah surely creates all these disasters as "warnings" to mankind. He is exalted in power and He has power over all things. Allah testifies to this in the verse: "He has power to send calamities on you, from above and below." (Surat al-An'am: 65) That there are so many serious physical threats around the world no doubt underlines one important reality. With disasters, in only a matter of seconds Allah may take back whatever He has granted man. Catastrophes may strike anywhere at any time. This is a clear demonstration that no place exists on earth that can guarantee man's security. Allah says this in the following verse:

Do the people of the towns feel secure against the coming of Our wrath by night while they are asleep? Or else, do they feel secure against its coming in broad daylight while they play about (carefree)? Do they

Great surges of water (tsunamis) at times may ravage coastal cities.

In 1997-1998, "El-Niño" raged over many cities. The total damage all over the world was put at 20 billion dollars.[8] (Above) A city affected by El-Niño Although water is of great significance for life on earth, devastating floods remain to be a threat. (Next) A house sunk in water.

then feel secure against the plan of Allah But no-one can, (unwisely), feel secure from the plan of Allah, except those (doomed) to ruin! (Surat al-A'raf: 97-99)

Water, granted to man as a favour, may in times turn out a disaster by the will of Allah. It is incomprehensible that man witnesses one or two floods every year and still disregards the possibility of experiencing such a calamity himself.

Ice falling at close to 100 miles an hour shattered automobile windows in Tampa, Florida, during a 1992 thunderstorm that cost some 25 million dollars in property damage.[9] The roof of a house damaged by hailstones.

Wildfires and fires caused by human neglect may cause major losses.

Natural Hazards and Disasters

An arsonist's blaze in the parched canyon above Laguna Beach, California triggered the worst urban wildfire of 1993. The inferno torched some 14,000 acres and 441 houses. The Mystic Hills neighbourhood was worst hit, with 286 homes turned to ashes.[10]

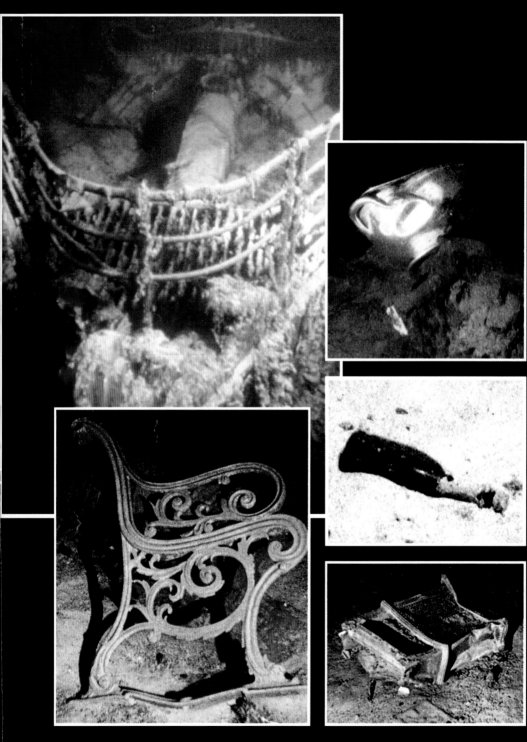

Some furniture and objects used aboard the Titanic. Together with the ocean liner, all these properties were buried in the depths of the ocean. Today,
very few people in the world remember the owners of these goods.

A Lesson from History: The Titanic

History abounds with cases of people relying on technological break-throughs and totally disregarding the might of Allah. That is exactly why many disasters have gone down in history as painful lessons for everyone. Each one of these events is important in the sense that it reminds man that neither wealth nor power, science nor technology has any power to resist the will of Allah.

Numerous examples of such incidents can be given. The best known is the famous Titanic, a huge ocean liner 55 meters in height and 275 meters in length, which sank nearly ninety years ago. The Titanic, intended to be an "assault on nature", was a grand project that employed a team of engineers and as many as five thousand people. Almost everybody was absolutely convinced that this ship would never sink. The ocean liner was a masterpiece of technology with many engineering advances that pushed back the limits of its day. Yet those who relied on the technical prowess of the ship did not take into consideration one important fact stated in the verse "The command of Allah is a decree that is made absolute" (Surat al-Ahzab 38) and that everyone will sooner or later meet his fate. Eventually, a minor failure led to the sinking of the ship and advanced technology could not save the Titanic from her bitter end.

From what the survivors of Titanic related, the majority of her passengers gathered on the deck to pray when they realised the ship was about to sink. In many sections of the Qur'an, this tendency of human behaviour is repeated. In times of serious trouble and danger, man sincerely prays and seeks the help of his Creator. However, when delivered from danger, they immediately turn away in ungratefulness:

> Your Lord is He that made the ship go smoothly for you through the sea, in order that you may seek of his bounty. For He is unto you most Merciful. When distress seizes you at sea, those that you call upon – beside Him – leave you in the lurch! But when He brings you back safe to land, you turn away (from Him). Most ungrateful is man! Do you then feel secure that He will not cause you to be swallowed up beneath the earth when you are on land, or that He will not send against you a violent tornado (with showers of stones) so that you shall find no-one to carry out your affairs for you? Or do

you feel secure that He will not send you back a second time to sea and send against you a heavy gale to drown you because of your ingratitude, so that you find no helper therein against Us? (Surat al-Isra: 66- 69)

One might never have experienced such a disaster, yet one should always remember that, at any time, one may find life stripped to its fundamentals. Accordingly, man should always occupy himself with the remembrance of Allah since "the power is wholly Allah's." (Surat al-Baqarah: 165) On the other hand, once a catastrophe strikes, one might not have the opportunity to change his ungrateful attitude towards Allah and seek to repent to Him. Death may be very sudden:

Do they see nothing in the government of the heavens and the earth and all that Allah has created? (Do they not see) that it may well be that their terms are nigh drawing to an end? In what message after this will they then believe? (Surat al-A'raf: 185)

By the Mercy of Allah

Each one of them We seized for his crime: against some of them We sent a violent tornado (with showers of stones); some were caught by a (mighty) blast; some We caused the earth to swallow up; and some We drowned (in the waters): It was not Allah who injured (or oppressed) them; They injured (and oppressed) their own souls. (Surat al-'Ankabut: 40)

What has been discussed so far is intended to remind those who forget their purpose in creation of an important fact: everything on earth owes its existence to Allah, the Creator who has created the entire material universe. In other words, everything's existence is consequent upon the exercise of the will of Allah. Therefore, nothing has a being separate and apart from Allah. The Qur'an tells us that nothing is beyond Allah's control: **"Allah has full power and control over His affair; but most of mankind know it not."** (Surah Yusuf: 21)

Nevertheless, as Allah makes clear in the second part of the verse, the majority of people are not aware of this. They assume, during the course of their lives, that no misfortune whatsoever will befall them, never thinking that they too are vulnerable to any of those devastating disasters. We feel that "others" experience such terrifying incidents and that "we" will always live in safety. News about disasters, accidents or epidemics surely makes us feel sympathy for the sufferers. We indeed share their sorrow; however, as disasters recede into memory, we become less concerned and such an attitude proves to be a passing interest for us. Once we immerse ourselves in the flow of daily life or face personal problems, we quickly develop a sense of apathy and remain indifferent to those who have been through disaster.

Nevertheless, the notion that every day of one's life will be the same is a flawed one. This is evident from the warnings of Allah. Certainly, those people who were exposed to various disasters did not know that a natural hazard would throw their life into complete disarray. They certainly started that day as an ordinary one, thinking that it would be the same as the preceding ones. However, it turned out to be totally different. Most probably, it never occurred to them that, on that particular day there would be a drastic change in their lives, which would transform life into a dangerous struggle. On such occasions, lives are reduced to their simplest truths. Surely, this is how Allah reminds man that security in this world is a sham.

A majority of people pay no heed to this, however. They forget that life is short and temporary and disregard that they will be judged in the presence of Allah. In this state of heedlessness, they spend their lives in pursuit of vain desires instead of living for the good pleasure of Allah.

Viewed from this standpoint, troubles are a mercy of Allah. Allah demonstrates the true nature of this world and encourages man to be prepared for the next life. That is why what is said to be a misfortune is in fact an opportunity offered by Allah. These misfortunes are given to people so that they may seek to repent and amend their conduct. The lessons that should be drawn from disasters are related in one of the verses:

> See they not that they are tried every year once or twice? Yet they turn not in repentance, and they take no heed. (Surat at-Tawbah: 126)

Past Civilisations

ut how many (countless) generations before them have We destroyed? Can you find a single one of them (now) or hear (so much as) a whisper of them? (Surah Maryam: 98)

Man is on earth to be tested. Throughout history, the pure messages and the revelations of Allah communicated to people by His messengers provided guidance for mankind. These messengers and books always summoned man to the right path, the path of Allah. Today, the last book of Allah, His only unaltered revelation to mankind is available: the Qur'an.

In the Qur'an, Allah informs us that He showed the right path to all people throughout world history and warned them through His messengers of the day of judgement and hell. However, a majority of these people denounced the prophets sent to them and showed animosity towards them. Because of their arrogance, they brought Allah's wrath down upon themselves and were quite suddenly wiped off the face of the earth. The relevant verse follows:

> As also 'Ad and Thamud, and the Companions of the Rass, and many a generation between them. To each one, We set forth parables and examples; and each one We broke to utter annihilation (for their wrong actions). And the (disbelievers) must indeed have passed by the town on which was rained a shower of evil: did they not then see it (with their own eyes)? But they fear not the Resurrection. (Surat al-Furqan: 38-40)

The news of previous peoples, which constitutes a great part of the Qur'an, is certainly one of the issues of the revelation to be contemplated. The lessons that are to be drawn from their experience is stated as follows in the Qur'an:

> See they not how many of those before them We did destroy? Generations We had established on the earth, in strength such as We have not given to you, for whom We poured out rain from the skies in abundance, and gave (fertile) streams flowing beneath their (feet): yet for their wrong actions We destroyed them, and raised in their wake fresh generations (to succeed them). (Surat al-An'am: 6)

Another verse addressed to men of understanding who can take warning and take heed is the following:

> But how many generations before them did We destroy (for their wrong actions), stronger in power than they? Then did they wander through the land: was there any place of escape (for them)? Verily in this is a message for any that has a heart and understanding or who gives ear and earnestly witnesses (the truth). (Surah Qaf: 36-37)

Allah in the Qur'an tells us that these cases of destruction should be a warning for succeeding generations. Nearly all the destructions of ancient peoples related in the Qur'an are identifiable, thanks to current archive studies and archaeological finds, and thus can be studied. Yet it would be a great mistake to develop only a historical or scientific approach while examining traces of these cases in the Qur'an. As stated in the following verse, each of these incidents is a warning from which to draw lessons:

> So, We made it an example to their own time and to their posterity, and a lesson to those who fear Allah. (Surat al-Baqarah: 66)

Yet, we should consider one significant fact: those communities who resisted obeying the commands of Allah did not suffer under Allah's wrath suddenly. Allah sent them messengers to warn them so that they would regret their behaviour and submit to Him. That all troubles befalling men is a reminder for the grievous punishment in the hereafter is stated in the Qur'an:

> And verily We make them taste the lower punishment before the greater, that happily they may return. (Surat as-Sajdah: 21)

Destruction often followed when these warnings evoked no response in the communities and when their perversity increased. All these communities were punished by the wrath of Allah. They disappeared from the pages of history and were replaced by new generations. These communities actually received benefit from the favours of Allah, led their lives in prosperity, indulged in the enjoyment of all sorts of pleasures and, while doing all these things, never occupied themselves with the remembrance of Allah. They never reflected on the fact that everything in this world is doomed to extinction. They savoured the moment and never thought about death and beyond. To them, anything and everything to do with worldly life seemed eternal. Yet, the real eternal life lies beyond death. They had no gain whatsoever from this perception of life; however, history provides sufficient evidence of their bitter destruction. Despite the passage of thousands of years, their memories remain as a warning, reminding current generations of the ends of those who stray from their Creator's path.

Thamud

Thamud are one of those communities that perished due to insolence towards divine revelation and overlooking the warnings of Allah. As stated in the Qur'an, Thamud were known for their prosperity and power and they were a nation who excelled in art.

> And remember how He made you inheritors after 'Ad and gave you habitations in the land: you build for yourselves palaces and castles in (open) plains, and carve out homes in the mountains; so bring to remembrance the benefits (you have received) from Allah, and refrain from evil and mischief on the earth. (Surat al-A'raf: 74)

In another verse, the social environment of Thamud is illustrated as follows:

> Will you be left secure, in (the enjoyment of) all that you have here? Gardens and springs, and cornfields and date-palms with spathes near breaking (with the weight of fruit)? And you carve houses out of (rocky) mountains with great skill. (Surat ash-Shu'ara: 146-149)

Exulting in affluence, Thamud led an extravagant life. In the Qur'an, Allah says that the prophet Salih was sent to Thamud to warn them. The prophet Salih was a person who was well-known among Thamud. His people, who did not expect him to proclaim the religion of truth, were surprised by his calling them to abandon the perversity they were in. A small part of the community complied with Salih's summons, but most did not accept what he said. In particular, the leaders of the community denied Salih and were antagonistic towards him. They tried to injure those who believed in Salih and to oppress them. They were enraged against Salih because he called them to worship Allah. This rage was not specific to

The Nabataeans, which was an Arab tribe, had established a kingdom in the Rum Valley in Jordan. In this place, also called the Valley of Petra, it is possible to see the best examples of the stone-carving work of these people. Also in the Qur'an, Thamud are mentioned with their mastery of masonry. However, today, what is left of both of these communities is some remains that give us an idea of the art of that time. In the pictures, various examples of the stone-carving work in Petra Valley are seen.

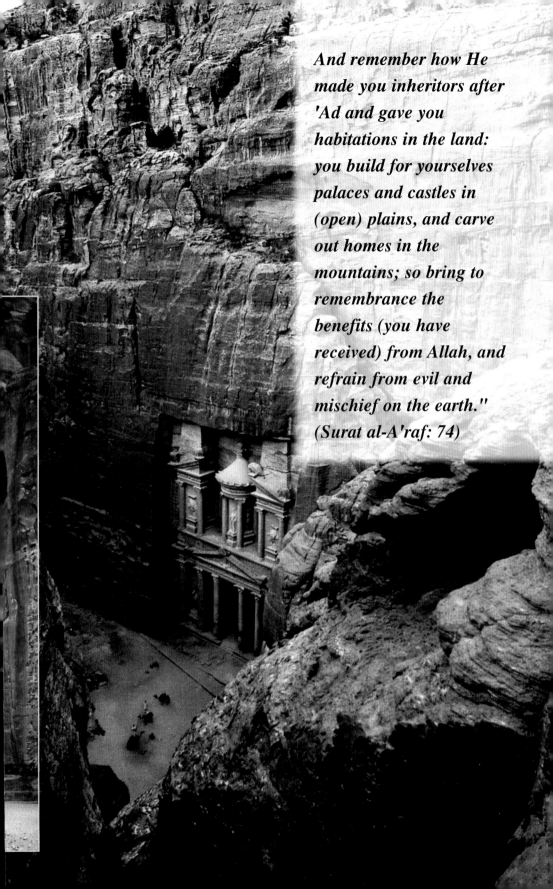

*And remember how He made you inheritors after 'Ad and gave you habitations in the land: you build for yourselves palaces and castles in (open) plains, and carve out homes in the mountains; so bring to remembrance the benefits (you have received) from Allah, and refrain from evil and mischief on the earth."
(Surat al-A'raf: 74)*

Thamud: they were repeating the mistake made by the people of Nuh and 'Ad who preceded them in history. This is why the Qur'an refers to these three peoples as follows:

> Has not the story reached you, (O people!), of those who (went) before you? Of the people of Nuh, and 'Ad and Thamud? And of those who (came) after them? None knows them but Allah. To them came messengers with clear (signs); but they put their hands up to their mouths, and said: "We deny (the mission) on which you have been sent, and we are really in suspicious (disquieting) doubt as to that to which you invite us." (Surah Ibrahim: 9)

Thamud were determined to remain arrogant and never change their attitude towards the prophet Salih and even were making plans to kill him. Salih warned them further saying: "Will you be left secure, in (the enjoyment of) all that you have here?" (Surat ash-Shu'ara: 146-149) Indeed, the Thamud increased their perversity being unaware of the penalty of Allahand adressed prophet Salid with pride and exultation:

> "O Salih! Bring about your threats, if you are a messenger (of Allah)!" (Surat al-A'raf: 77).

The prophet Salih told them, by Allah's revelation, that they would be perished in three days.

Three days later, the prophet Salih's warning came true and Thamud perished.

> The (mighty) blast overtook the wrongdoers, and they lay prostrate in their homes before the morning, as if they had never dwelt or flourished there. Ah! Behold! For Thamud rejected their Lord and Cherisher! Ah! Behold! Removed (from sight) were Thamud! (Surah Hud: 67-68)

Thamud paid dearly, by being destroyed, for not obeying their messenger. The buildings they had constructed and the works of art they had produced could not protect them from the penalty. Thamud were destroyed with a grievous penalty just like all the other peoples who have denied faith before and after them. In brief, their ends matched their attitude. Those who revolted were utterly ruined, and those who obeyed received eternal deliverance.

The People of Saba

The story of the people of Saba (Sheba in the Bible) is recounted in the Qur'an as follows:

> There was, for Saba, aforetime, a sign in their homeland – two Gardens to the right and to the left. "Eat of the Sustenance (provided) by your Lord, and be grateful to Him: a territory fair and happy, and a Lord Oft-Forgiving!"But they turned away (from Allah), and We sent against them the Flood (released) from the dams, and We converted their two garden (rows) into "gardens" producing bitter fruit, and tamarisks, and some few (stunted) Lote-trees. That was the requital We gave them because they ungratefully rejected faith: and never do We give (such) requital except to such as are ungrateful rejecters. (Surah Saba: 15-17)

As related in the verses above, the people of Saba lived in a region noted for its arrestingly beautiful and fruitful vineyards and gardens. In such a country, where living standards and circumstances were so high, what they should have done was be grateful to Allah. Yet, as stated in the verse, they "turned away from Allah". Because they laid claim to all their prosperity, they lost it all. As we are informed by the verse, the Arim flood laid waste the whole country.

The Ma'rib Dam was a work of a very advanced technology. Yet the dam collapsed and the "Arim flood" laid waste to the people of Saba and their land.

The Glorious Sumerians

Sumer was a collection of city-states around the lower Tigris and Euphrates in what is now southern Iraq. In our day, the terrain that some-one travelling to southern Iraq would most frequently encounter is nothing but vast desert. Most of the land, with the exception of cities, and

Queen Puabi may have been buried together with treasures beyond counting, but that did not save her body from being reduced to a skeleton.

regions that have since been afforested, is covered with sand. These deserts, once the homeland of the Sumerians, have been there for thousands of years. Their glorious country, which today we are likely to meet only in textbooks, was as real as any contemporary civilisation. These people were as alive as we are today and they created architectural masterpieces. In a sense, the magnificent cities built by the Sumerians are part of the cultural heritage of our own time.

Among what survives of the cultural remains of the Sumerians, we have information about an elaborate funeral held for Puabi, one of their queens. Vivid accounts of this splendid ceremony are to be found in a number of sources and they tell us that the dead body of the queen was embellished in an extraordinary way. Her corpse was dressed in cloth fashioned from beads of silver, gold and precious stones, and with tassels of pearls. On its head was a wig decorated with a crown encrusted with golden leaves. A vast amount of gold was also placed in the tomb.[11]

In brief, Queen Puabi, an important name in Sumerian history, was buried with a splendid treasure. According to accounts, these matchless riches were carried to her tomb by a procession of guards and servants. Queen Puabi may have been buried together with treasures beyond counting, but that did not save her body from being reduced to a skeleton.

Like all other people in her kingdom, for whom she may have felt contempt because they were poor, her body decayed under the ground becoming a putrefying mass of bacteria. This is surely an impressive example showing that the wealth and properties of this world by no means ensure salvation from a disastrous end.

The Minoans

Land and sea may lie relatively still for centuries. Then, an upheaval suddenly unleashes a cataclysm. Perhaps no event illustrates such a horror so clearly as the calamity of ancient Thera. What happened there may have been the most explosive volcanic eruption in history. Towering over the Aegean Sea some 3,500 years ago, a mile-high volcano formed a ten-mile-wide island. There loomed over a magnificent civilisation centred some seventy miles to the south on the island of Crete. At its peak, perhaps 30,000 people dwelled in Akrotiri, Thera's main city, in which were erected fresco-decorated palaces and from which were dispatched ships laden with goods for trade. While scholars remain uncertain of the exact date – estimates range from 1470 to 1628 BCE – they know the sequence of events. Light earth tremors were followed by a violent quake, aftershocks, and an explosion whose reverberations were audible as far as Scandinavia, the Persian Gulf, and the Rock of Gibraltar.[12] Huge tidal waves arched up and smashed Amnisos, the harbour of Knossos. Today, only the remains of those glorious palaces are left.

The Minoan civilisation, one of the most important civilisations of the period, most probably never expected such a drastic end. Those people who boasted of their wealth and properties lost everything they had. Allah, in the Qur'an, underlines that the drastic ends of such ancient civilisations should be reflected on by contemporary societies:

> Does it not teach them a lesson, how many generations We destroyed before them, in whose dwellings they (now) go to and fro? Verily in that are Signs: Do they not then listen? (Surat as-Sajdah: 26)

The Disaster of Pompeii

For historians the remains of Pompeii are striking testimony to the debauchery that once prevailed there. Even the streets of Pompeii, a symbol of the degeneration of the Roman Empire, evoke the enjoyment and pleasure indulged in by this city: the once busy streets lined with taverns, night-clubs, and brothels, still provide glimpses that the disaster left of the daily life.

Here, on soil now enriched with volcanic ash, were once prosperous farms, lush vineyards and luxurious summerhouses. Situated between the slopes of Vesuvius and the sea, Pompeii was the favourite summer resort of wealthy Romans who had escaped the sweltering capital. Yet, Pompeii witnessed one of the most fearsome volcanic eruptions in history, obliterating the town from the face of the earth. Today, the remains of the inhabitants of this city – asphyxiated by the poisonous vapours of Vesuvius as they were going about their daily lives as usual – vividly portray details pertaining to the Roman way of life. The disaster struck Pompeii, together with the neighbouring city Herculaneum, on a summer day, just at a time when the region was crowded with wealthy Romans spending the season in their glorious villas.

The date was the 24th August 79CE. Investigations at the site reveal that the eruption progressed in discrete stages. Before the eruption, the region was shaken several times. Distant, high-pitched rumblings, deep and terrible, coming from the volcano, accompanied these quakes. At first, Vesuvius ejected a column of steam and ash. "Then this roiling cloud rose high into the atmosphere carrying pieces of old rock torn from the volcano's conduit and millions of tons of fresh, glassy pumice. Prevailing winds carried the ash cloud toward Pompeii, where 'small stones' began to fall. As the sun-extinguishing canopy extended over the city, pumice and ash rained down on Pompeii, accumulating at the rate of six inches an hour."[13]

Herculaneum was closer to Vesuvius; most of its residents fled the city terrified by the fast-moving pyroclastic surge that roared towards them. Those who did not leave the city immediately, did not live long to regret their delay. The pyroclastic surge on reaching Herculaneum killed these tarriers while a slower-moving pyroclastic flow engulfed the town, burying it. Excavations at Pompeii, on the other hand, reveal that a majority of its inhabitants were reluctant to leave the city. They thought they were not in danger because Pompeii was not very close to the crater. For this reason, most wealthy Pompeiians did not abandon their homes and instead took refuge in their houses and shops, hoping the tempest would soon blow over. They all perished before they had time to realise that it was too late. In just one day, Pompeii and Herculaneum along with six nearby villages were wiped off the map. The Qur'an declares that events such as these are a reminder to all:

> These are some of the stories of communities that We relate to you: of them, some are standing, and some have been mown down (by the sickle of time). (Surah Hud: 100)

Pompeii, a place of splendour and beauty, perished together with its twenty thousand inhabitants.

Unravelling the secrets of Pompeii was not possible until centuries later. Rather than mere clues however, the excavations of the ancient city yielded up vivid representations of its people's daily lives. The shapes of many of the agonised victims were preserved intact. The related verse follows:

> Such is the chastisement of your Lord when He chastises communities in the midst of their wrong: grievous, indeed, and severe is His chastisement. (Surah Hud: 102)

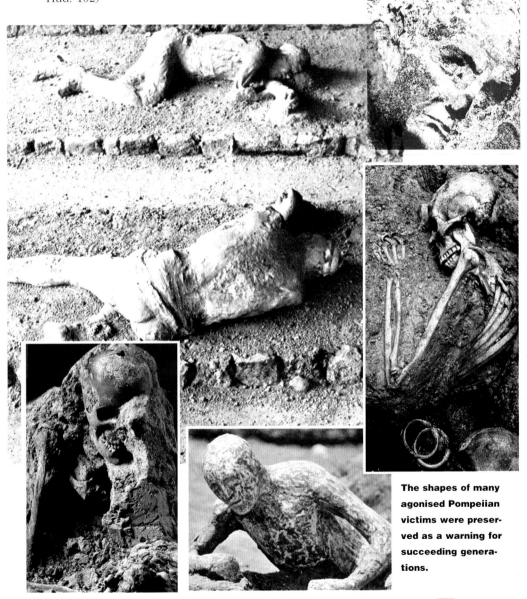

The shapes of many agonised Pompeiian victims were preserved as a warning for succeeding generations.

Today, vast ruins are humbling evidence of complex civilisations that once flourished hundreds, even thousand of years ago. Many of the builders of the great metropolises from different epochs of history are now nameless. Their wealth, technology or works of art did not save them from a bitter end. It was not them but succeeding generations who took advantage of their rich heritage. With few clues to guide us, the origins and fates of these ancient civilisations are mysteries to this day. Yet two things are evident: they assumed they would never die and they indulged in worldly pleasures. They left behind great monuments believing that thereby they would achieve immortality. No less than these ancient civilisations, many groups of people today also have such a mindset. In expectation of immortalising their names, a majority of the members of modern societies devote themselves entirely to accumulating more wealth or to creating works to leave behind. Moreover, it is more than likely that they revel in more extravagance than did earlier generations and remain heedless of Allah's revelations. There are many lessons to be drawn from the social attitudes and experiences of ancient communities. None of those early communities survived. The works of art and monuments they left behind may have helped them be remembered by succeeding generations but they did not save them from divine punishment or prevent their corpses from decaying. Their remains stand there only as a reminder and warning of Allah's wrath on those who are rebellious and ungrateful for the riches bestowed by Him.

Undoubtedly the lessons to be drawn from such historical events should eventually lead to wisdom. Only then can one comprehend that what befell early societies was not purposeless. One may further realise that only Almighty Allah has the power to create any disaster at any moment. The world is a place where man is being tested. Those who submit to Allah will attain salvation. Those who are satisfied with this world, on the other hand, will be deprived of a blessed eternity. No doubt, their ends will match their deeds and they will be judged in accordance with their deeds. Surely, Allah is the Best of Judges.

Man's True Abode: Hereafter

Many people assume that it is possible to lead a perfect life in this world. According to this view, a happy and satisfactory life is attainable through material prosperity, which along with a fulfilling home life and recognition of one's social status are generally regarded as the fundamentals of a perfect life.

Yet according to the Qur'anic point of view, a "perfect life" – that is, one without any problems – is never possible in this world. That is simply because life in the world is deliberately designed to be imperfect.

The origin of the Arabic word for 'world' – dunya – has a significant meaning. Etymologically, it is derived from the root daniy, which means "simple", "inferior", "low" and "worthless". Hence, the word 'world' in Arabic inherently comprises these qualities.

The insignificance of this life is emphasised many times earlier in this book. Indeed, all factors believed to make life wonderful – wealth, personal and business success, marriage, children, and so on – are nothing but vain deceptions. The related verse follows:

> Know you (all), that the life of this world is but play and amusement, pomp and mutual boasting and multiplying (in rivalry) among yourselves, riches and children. Here is a similitude: How rain and the growth which it brings forth, delight (the hearts of) the tillers; soon it withers; you will see it grow yellow; then it becomes dry and crumbles away. But in the Hereafter is a penalty severe (for the devotees of wrong). And forgiveness from Allah and (His) good pleasure (for the devotees of Allah). And what is the life of this

world, but goods and chattels of deception? (Surat al-Hadid: 20)

In another verse, Allah gives an account of the inclination felt by man for the world rather than the hereafter:

Nay (behold), you prefer the life of this world, but the hereafter is better and more enduring. (Surat al-A'la: 16-17)

Problems arise only because, rather than the hereafter, people value this life too highly. They are pleased and content with what they have here in this world. Such an attitude means nothing more than turning one's face away from the promise of Allah and consequently from the reality of His mighty existence. Allah proclaims that a grievous end awaits them:

Those who expect not the meeting with Us but desire the life of the world and feel secure therein, and those who are neglectful of Our revelations... (Surah Yunus: 7)

Of course, the imperfection of this life does not gainsay the fact that there are also good and beautiful things on earth. But here on earth, what is regarded as beautiful, delightful, pleasing and attractive stands cheek-by-jowl with the imperfect, flawed and ugly. In this world, good and evil are commingled. This is but a reminder of paradise and hell. Indeed, if observed with a sound and conscientious mind, these facts would make a person realise the truth of the hereafter. With Allah, that life which is deemed good and beneficial for man is actually that of the hereafter.

Allah commands His faithful servants to make serious efforts to attain paradise in the verse below:

Be quick in the race for forgiveness from your Lord, and for Paradise whose width is that (of the whole) of the heavens and of the earth, prepared for the righteous. (Surat Ali-'Imran: 133)

Those who Hasten for Paradise

In the Qur'an, believers are given the glad tidings of an eternal reward and happiness. Yet, what is commonly disregarded is the fact that this happiness and eternal pleasure start when we are still in this life. That is because, in this world too, believers are not deprived of the favours and benevolence of Allah.

In the Qur'an, Allah states that true believers who engage in good deeds in this world will find an excellent dwelling in the Hereafter:

> Whoever does right actions, man or woman, and has faith, verily, to him will We give a new life, a life that is good and pure and We will bestow on such their reward according to the best of their actions. (Surah an-Nahl: 97)

As a reward and source of bliss, in this world Allah bestows many favours as well as unprecedented opportunities for personally and socially fulfilling lives to His true servants. This is the immutable law of Allah. Since wealth, splendour and beauty are the fundamental characteristics of paradise, Allah opens His fortunes to His sincere believers also in this world. This is certainly the beginning of a comfortable and honourable life that will never end.

Beautiful places and ornaments in this world are but imperfect echoes of the real ones in paradise. Their existence makes true believers think of paradise and feel a deeper longing for it. On the other hand, all through his life, it is entirely possible that a believer may suffer serious trouble and grief; yet true believers put their trust in Allah and patiently bear up under any sorrows befalling them. Furthermore, being aware that this is a way to attain the good pleasure of Allah, such an attitude affords a special relief to their hearts.

A believer is someone who is constantly aware of the existence of his Creator. He complies with His commands and is careful to lead the kind of life described in the Qur'an. He has realistic expectations and hopes for his life after death. Since a believer puts his trust in his Creator, Allah relieves his heart of all misery and suffering.

What is more important, a believer, at every moment, feels the guidance and support of his Creator. This is actually a peaceful state of mind and heart that is a consequence of knowing that Allah is with him every time he prays, engages in good deeds, or does something – important or insignificant – solely to attain His good pleasure.

This is certainly a feeling of security inspiring the heart of a believer who comprehends that "for him are angels ranged before him and behind him who guard him by Allah's command" (Surat ar-Ra'd: 11), and that he will be victorious in his struggle in the name of Allah, and that he will receive the good news of an eternal reward: paradise. Hence, true believers never fear or grieve, in accordance with the inspiration of Allah to angels "I am with you: give firmness to the Believers." (Surat al-Anfal: 12)

Believers are those who say "Our Lord is Allah and, further, stand straight and steadfast." (Surah Fussilat: 30). They are also "those upon whom the angels descend" and to whom the angels say "fear not nor grieve, but hear good tidings of the paradise which you are promised." (Surah Fussilat: 30). Believers are also aware that their Creator "places no burden on any soul but that which it can bear." (Surat al-A'raf: 42). They are well aware that "Allah is the One who has created all in proportion and measure." (Surat al-Qamar: 49). Hence, they are the ones who say "Nothing will happen to us except what Allah has decreed for us: He is our protector." (Surat at-Tawbah: 51) and put their trust in Allah. "No harm touched them" since they say "Allah is sufficient for us and most excellent is the Protector." (Surat Ali-'Imran: 173-174). Yet, since the world is a place of testing for all human beings, believers will necessarily be confronted by some difficulties. Hunger, thirst, loss of property, disease, accidents and so on may also strike them at any time. Poverty as well as many other kinds of trouble or affliction may also befall them. The kind of test a believer may go through is described as follows in the Qur'an:

> Or do you think that you shall enter Paradise without such (trials) as came to those who passed away before you? They encountered suffering and adversity, and were so shaken in spirit that even the Messenger and those of faith who were with him cried: "When (will come) the help of Allah?" Ah! Verily, the help of Allah is (always) near! (Surat al-Baqarah: 214)

Of course adversities never altered the respect and fear the Prophet, and his Companions had for Allah. No alteration in their attitude ever occurred when they faced trouble. Allah, also, gives the glad tidings of His support to believers in the verse: "Ah! Verily, the help of Allah is (always) near." In consequence, "but Allah will deliver the right acting to their place of salvation: no evil shall touch them, nor shall they grieve." (Surat az-Zumar: 61)

Believers are aware that difficult times are specially created and that their responsibility is to respond to them with patience and constancy. Furthermore these are great opportunities to show one's perseverance and commitment to Allah and are a means to attain personal maturity in His sight. Thus, a believer becomes happier, excited and more committed on such occasions.

However, the attitude of disbelievers is totally different. Difficult times make them fall into despair. Apart from physical pain, a disbeliever also suffers from great mental distress.

The fear, hopelessness, pessimism, grief, worry, anxiety and agitation that are the characteristic traits of disbelievers in this world are but pale versions of the real pain from which they will suffer in the Hereafter. Allah "makes their breast close and constricted, as if they had to climb up to the skies and thus Allah (heaps) the penalty on those who refuse to believe." (Surah al-An'am: 125)

On the other hand, those true believers that seek forgiveness and repent to Allah are the recipients of the benevolence and favours of Allah in this world as related in the following verse:

> (And to preach thus), "Seek you the forgiveness of your Lord, and turn to Him in repentance; that He may grant you enjoyment, good (and true), for a term appointed, and bestow His abounding grace on all who abound in merit! But if you turn away, then I fear for you the penalty of a great day." (Surah Hud: 3)

In another verse, the life of believers is described as follows:

> To the righteous (when) it is said, "What is it that your Lord has revealed?" They say "All that is good." To those who do good, there is good in this world, and the Home of the Hereafter is even better and excellent indeed is the Home of the righteous. (Surat an-Nahl: 30)

The Hereafter is surely superior to and better than this world. Compared to the Hereafter, this world is but a mean and entirely worthless place. Hence, if a person wants to set a goal for himself, that goal should be paradise in the Hereafter. It should also be remembered that those who seek paradise receive the benevolence of their Creator in this world as well. But those who seek this world in rebellion against Allah often attain nothing of worth from it and then their abode in the next life is hell.

Paradise

Allah promises paradise to those who come to His presence as believers. Surely, Allah does not fail to keep His promise. People whose faith is assured, know that their Creator will keep His promise and that they will be accepted in paradise provided that they live as true believers in this world:

> Paradise of Eternity, those which (Allah) Most Gracious has promised to His slaves in the Unseen: for His promise must (necessarily) come to pass. (Surah Maryam: 61)

The moment of entering paradise is the most important time for the faithful who believe and do good deeds. All through their lives, they strove for it, prayed for it and performed right actions to obtain it. In the presence of Allah, it is surely the best place to stay and the real place to attain: paradise, the place specially prepared for believers. Allah describes this unique moment in the following verse:

> Gardens of perpetual bliss: they shall enter there, as well as the righteous among their fathers, their spouses, and their offspring. And angels shall enter unto them from every gate (with the salutation): "Peace unto you for that you persevered in patience! Now how excellent is the final home!" (Surat ar-Rad: 23-24)

The Beauty of Paradise

> The parable of Paradise which the righteous are promised! Beneath it flow rivers: perpetual is the enjoyment thereof and the shade therein. Such is the end of the righteous; and the end of disbelievers is hell. (Surat ar-Ra'd: 35)

An excellent vista of lakes, rivers, and lush greenery is the sort of paradise imagined by the ordinary person. However this image of paradise needs to be clarified because it does not accurately reflect the Qur'anic point of view. It is certainly true that paradise has significant natural beauty; yet, such a pleasant atmosphere only portrays its appealing and aesthetic aspects. That is why in the Qur'an there are references to splendid mansions, shady gardens, and flowing rivers. However limiting paradise to physical magnificence will definitely prove to be inadequate to the reality.

The beauty and glory of paradise are beyond one's imagination. The Qur'anic words "containing all kinds (of delights)" (Surat ar-Rahman: 48) surely illustrate a vivid picture of the real nature of paradise. What is meant by "delights" are things specially created by Allah the All-Knowing. These delights may well be surprising rewards or things in which to take such pleasure as human beings have never imagined. The promise of Allah "they shall have, before their Lord, all that they wish for. That will indeed be the magnificent bounty (of Allah)" (Surat ash-Shura: 22) makes it explicit that, as a favour of Allah, the imagination of believers will shape a Paradise according to their own tastes and wishes.

The Eternal Residence of Believers

> Allah has promised to believers, men and women, gardens under which rivers flow, to dwell therein, and beautiful mansions in gardens of everlasting bliss. But the greatest bliss is the good pleasure of Allah: that is the supreme felicity. (Surat at-Tawbah: 72)

In this world, believers live "in houses, which Allah has permitted to be raised to honour; for the celebration, in them, of His name." (Surat an-Nur: 36) By Allah's command, these residences are kept clean and especially cared for.

Similar to them are the residences in paradise; they are places where Allah is glorified and His name is constantly remembered.

As well as grand mansions in beautiful spots, believers' residences in the world can be works of ultra-modern design and architecture, built in beautiful cities.

The residences in paradise described in the Qur'an, are usually located in natural beauties:

> But it is for those who fear their Lord that lofty mansions, one above another, have been built: beneath them flow rivers (of delight). (Such is) the Promise of Allah. Never does Allah fail in (His) promise. (Surat az-Zumar: 20)

The mansions, mentioned in the verse, below which rivers flow, may have wide windows or halls surrounded with glass walls making it possible to watch this beautiful scene. These are beautifully decorated houses with thrones specially designed for the comfort of the believers. They will and various kinds of drinks. The design and decoration of the mansions are of the best quality of textiles and materials. Comfortable couches lined with silk brocade and thrones are specially emphasised in many verses:

> They will be on thrones encrusted with gold and precious stones, reclining on them, facing each other. (Surat al-Waqi'ah: 15-16)
>
> They will recline with ease on thrones of dignity arranged in ranks... (Surat at-Tur: 20)

As the verses also suggest, thrones are the symbols of dignity, splendour and wealth. Allah wants His servants to reside in such glorious places in paradise. In such magnificent surroundings, believers constantly keep remembering Allah and repeat His word:

> They will enter Gardens of Eden where they will be adorned with gold bracelets and pearls, and where their clothing will be of silk. They will say, 'Praise be to Allah, Who has removed from us (all) sorrow: for our Lord is indeed Oft-Forgiving, Ready to appreciate (service), Who has, out of His bounty, settled us in a Home that will last: no toil nor sense of weariness shall touch us therein.' (Surat al-Fatir: 33-35)

The basic material of paradise is "works of great delicacy" and "remarkable beauties". These are all the reflections of the ultimate intelligence and art of Allah. For instance, thrones are encrusted with gold and precious stones. The thrones are not ordinary but exalted ones. Clothes are of silk and precious textile. Moreover, the silver and golden jewellery will be complementary to these precious garments. In the Qur'an, Allah gives many details of paradise, yet from those expressions it is clear that every believer will enjoy a Garden designed according to his own imagination. No doubt, Allah will bestow many other astonishing gifts on His beloved servants.

A Garden Beyond Imagination

> To them will be passed round, dishes and goblets of gold: there will be there all that the souls could desire, all that their eyes could delight in: and you shall abide therein timelessly, for ever. (Surat az-Zukhruf: 71)

From the descriptions and illustrations existing in the Qur'an, we can get a general understanding of what paradise is like. In the verse "Whenever they shall be given a portion of the fruit thereof, they shall say:

"Whenever they shall be given a portion of the fruit thereof, they shall say: 'This is what was given to us before,'" (Surat al-Baqarah: 25) Allah states that the favours in paradise will be fundamentally similar to those in this world. In accordance with the description of the verse "And admit them to the Paradise which He has announced for them," (Surah Muhammad: 6), we can arrive at the conclusion that Allah will let believers reside in a Paradise with which they were familiar before.

Nevertheless, any information that we may gather about paradise in this world must necessarily be inadequate; it can only give some hints with which to paint a general picture. "Here is a parable of the Paradise which the righteous are promised: in it are rivers of water incorruptible; rivers of milk of which the taste never changes; rivers of wine, a joy to those who drink; and rivers of honey pure and clear." (Surah Muhammad: 15). This verse makes it clear that paradise is a place beyond our imagination. In the human soul, this verse evokes the feeling that it is a place of unexpected sights.

On the other hand, Allah describes paradise as "an entertainment" or a "feast":

> But as to those who are careful of (their duty to) their Lord, they shall have gardens beneath which rivers flow, abiding in them; an entertainment from their Lord, and that which is with Allah is best for the righteous. (Surat Ali-'Imran: 198)

In this verse, Allah introduces paradise as a place of entertainment and joy. The "end" of this life, the joy of passing the "test" and attaining the best of places to reside for all eternity, are surely causes for believers to rejoice. This celebration will be a splendid one: one that bears no similarity whatsoever to any kind of feast or joy in this world. It is certain that it will be a celebration beyond the traditions and rituals of all customary shows, festivals, carnivals or feasts of preceding nations as well as nations of today.

In the eternal life, the fact that believers will enjoy various kinds of unceasing entertainment brings to mind another significant characteristic of believers in paradise: never feeling weariness. In the Qur'an, this condition is expressed as follows in words spoken by believers: "...Who has, out of

His Bounty, settled us in a Home that will last: neither toil nor sense of weariness shall touch us therein." (Surat al-Fatir: 35).

No doubt, believers will also not suffer from mental fatigue there. In contrast to paradise where "there no sense of fatigue shall touch them" (Surat al-Hijr 48), man in this world feels fatigue since his body has not been created strong. When one feels tired, it becomes difficult to concentrate and to make sound decisions. Due to weariness, one's perceptions alter. Yet, such a state of mind never exists in paradise. All senses remain keen perceiving the creation of Allah in the best manner. Believers are completely unaware of any feelings of fatigue and, hence, they taste the gifts of Allah without interruption. The pleasure and joy felt are boundless and eternal.

In an environment where fatigue and boredom do not exist, Allah rewards believers by creating "whatever they wish". Indeed, Allah gives the good news that He will create more than believers can imagine or wish: "There will be for them therein all that they wish – and more besides – in Our Presence." (Surah Qaf: 35)

It should be kept in mind that one of the most important favours of paradise is that "Allah will preserve believers from the Penalty of the Blazing Fire" (Surat ad-Dukhan: 56) and "not the slightest sound will they hear of Hell." (Surat al-Anbiya: 102)

Whenever they wish, on the other hand, believers have the opportunity to see and talk to the people of hell. They feel grateful for this favour also:

> Saying: "Surely we feared before on account of our families but Allah has been gracious to us and He has saved us from the punishment of the hot wind. Surely, we called upon Him before. Surely He is the Benign, the Merciful." (Surat at-Tur: 26-28)

Paradise is described in the Qur'an as follows: "And when you look, it is there you will see a Bliss and a Realm Magnificent." (Surat al-Insan: 20) Here, eyes savour and enjoy a different prospect, a different magnificence. Every corner and spot is decorated with precious ornaments. Such magnificence is only for those believers upon whom Allah bestows His mercy and to whom He grants His Garden. And We shall remove from their hearts any lurking sense of injury: (they will be) brothers joyfully facing each other on thrones of dignity. (Surat al-Hijr: 47) Abiding therein; they shall not desire removal from them. (Surat al-Kahf: 108)

The Most Important Favour of Allah: His Good Pleasure

Allah has promised to believers, men and women, gardens under which rivers flow, to dwell therein, and beautiful mansions in gardens of everlasting bliss. But the greatest bliss is the good pleasure of Allah: that is the supreme felicity. (Surat at-Tawbah: 72)

In the preceding pages, we mentioned the glorious favours that Allah bestows upon man in paradise. It is evident that paradise is a place containing all the joys man can experience through his five senses. However, the superior quality of paradise is the good pleasure of Allah. For believers, attaining the good pleasure of Allah becomes a major source of peace and joy in the hereafter. Furthermore, seeing the favours of Allah and being grateful to Allah for His benevolence makes them happy. In the Qur'an, the believers in paradise are described as follows:

...Allah is well pleased with them and they with Allah. That is the great salvation, (the fulfilment of all desires). (Surat al-Ma'idah: 119)

What makes the favours of paradise so precious is the good pleasure of Allah. The same types of favours may also exist in this world, yet if the good pleasure of Allah is not involved, believers do not enjoy these favours. This is a very important issue on which one needs to ponder. What actually makes a favour precious is something beyond the savour and pleasure it gives. What really matters, is the fact that Allah has bestowed that favour.

A believer who has the benefit of such a favour and is grateful to his Creator derives his main pleasure from knowing that it is the benevolence of Allah. The satisfaction can be found only from the fact that Allah protects him, loves him and that his Creator shows His Mercy to him. Therefore, one's heart only takes pleasure from paradise. He is created to be a servant of Allah and therefore he takes only pleasure from His benevolence.

That is why a "Heaven on earth" – the utopia of disbelievers – can never exist in this world. Even if everything existing in paradise were to be gathered and put into this world, it would still make no sense without the good pleasure of Allah.

In brief, paradise is a gift of Allah to His true servants and that is why it is important to them. Since "they are (but) slaves raised to honour," (Surat al-Anbiya: 26) they attain eternal happiness and joy. The words of the believers in paradise are "Blessed be the name of your Lord, full of Majesty, Bounty and Honour." (Surat ar-Rahman: 78)

Hell

The place, where disbelievers will remain for all eternity is specially created to give pain to the human body and soul. That is solely because the disbelievers are guilty of great wrong and Allah's justice entails punishment upon them.

Being ungrateful and rebellious to the Creator, the One who gives man a soul, is the greatest wrong action that can be committed in the whole universe. Therefore, in the hereafter there is grievous punishment for such a deadly wrong. That is what hell serves for. Man is created to be a servant of Allah. If he denies the main purpose of his creation, then he surely receives what he deserves. Allah states the following in one of the verses:

> ...those who are too arrogant to serve Me will surely find themselves in Hell – in humiliation! (Surat al-Ghafir: 60)

Since the majority of people will be sent to hell at the end and punishment in it is timeless and eternal, then the main aim, the basic goal of humanity should be to avoid hell. The biggest threat to man is hell and nothing can be more important than saving one's soul from it.

Despite this, almost all people on earth live in a state of unconsciousness. They occupy themselves with other troubles in their daily lives. They work for months, years, even decades for insignificant issues, yet never think of the biggest threat, the gravest danger to their eternal existence. Hell is right next to them; yet, they are too blind to see it:

> Closer and closer to mankind comes their Reckoning: yet they heed not and

they turn away. Never comes (aught) to them of a renewed Message from their Lord, but they listen to it as in jest, their hearts toying as with trifles. (Surat al-Anbiya: 1-3)

Such people engage in vain effort. They spend all their lives chasing after chimerical goals. Most of the time, their goals are being promoted in the company, marrying, having a "happy family life", earning a lot of money or being an advocate of a useless ideology. While doing these things, these people are unaware of the big threat ahead of them. For these people, hell is an imaginary fiction.

In fact, hell is more real than this world. The world will cease to exist after some time, but hell will remain for all eternity. Allah, the Creator of the universe and the world and all the delicate balances in nature, has likewise created the hereafter, paradise and hell. A grievous punishment is promised to all disbelievers and hypocrites:

Enough for them is Hell: In it they will burn, and evil is that destination. (Surat al-Mujadilah: 8)

Hell, the worst place that can ever be imagined, is a source of the sheerest torture. This torture and pain is not similar to any kind of pain in this world. It is much more intense than any pain or misery one can ever face in this world. It is surely the work of Allah, the Exalted in Wisdom.

A second reality about hell is that, for everyone, this torture is timeless and eternal. The majority of people in this ignorant society have a common misconception about hell: they assume that they will "serve their sentence" in hell for a certain period and that then they will be forgiven. This is only wishful thinking. This belief is also particularly widespread among those who assume themselves believers yet neglect to perform their duties towards Allah. They assume that they can indulge in worldly pleasures as much as possible. According to the same belief, they will attain paradise after receiving punishment in hell for a while. However, the end awaiting them is more painful than they expect. Hell is surely a place of everlasting torment. In the Qur'an, it is often stressed that punishment for disbelievers is constant and everlasting. The following verse makes this fact explicit:"They will dwell therein for ages." (Surat an-Naba: 23)

Being ungrateful and rebellious to the Creator who "gave hearing and sight and intelligence and affections" (Surat an-Nahl 78) certainly deserves unceasing suffering. The excuses one puts forth will not save one from hell. The verdict given for those who display indifference – or worse, animosity – to the religion of his Creator is certain and invariable. In the world, they were arrogant and avoided submitting to Almighty Allah. They were also bitter enemies of true believers. On the day of judgement, they will hear the following:

> So enter the gates of Hell, to dwell therein. Thus evil indeed is the abode of the arrogant. (Surat an-Nahl: 29)

The most fearsome characteristic of hell is its eternal nature. Once in hell, there will be no return. The only reality is hell together with many other kinds of torture. Encountering such an eternal torture, a person falls into desperate hopelessness. He has no further expectations. This state is described as follows in the Qur'an:

> As to those who are rebellious and wicked, their abode will be the Fire. Every time they wish to get away therefrom, they will be forced thereinto, and it will be said to them: "Taste you the Penalty of the Fire, which you were wont to reject as false." (Surat as-Sajdah: 20)

The Torments of Hell

> And (as for) those who disbelieve in Our signs, they are the people of the left hand. On them is fire closed over. (Surat al-Balad: 19-20)

On the day of judgement, there will be billions of people, yet this huge crowd will not give the disbelievers an opportunity to escape from the judgement. After the judgement of the disbelievers takes place in the presence of Allah, they will be labelled "the people of the left hand". This is the time when they will be sent to hell. From then on, they will bitterly comprehend that hell will be their permanent residence. Those sent to hell come with a witness and a driver:

> And the trumpet is blown; that is the day of the threatening. And every soul has come, with it a driver and a witness. Certainly you were heedless of it, but now We have removed from you your veil, so your sight today is sharp. And his companions shall say: "This is what is ready with me." Do cast into

Hell every ungrateful, rebellious one, forbidder of good, exceeder of limits, doubter, who sets up another god with Allah, so do cast him into severe chastisement.(Surat Qaf: 20-26)

Disbelievers are driven to this terrible place "in divisions". Yet, on the way to hell, the fear of it is inspired in the hearts of disbelievers. The horrible noise and roar of fire is heard from a distance:

When they are cast therein, they will hear the terrible drawing in of its breath even as it blazes forth almost bursting with fury. (Surat al-Mulk: 7-8)

From the verses, it is obvious that when they are recreated, all disbelievers will understand what will befall them. They remain alone; no friends, relatives, or supporters will be there to help. Disbelievers will not have the strength to be arrogant and they will lose all their self-confidence. They will look with averted eyes. One of the verses describes this moment as follows:

And you will see them brought forward to the (penalty), in a humble frame of mind because of (their) disgrace, (and) looking with a stealthy glance. And the believers will say: "Those are indeed in loss, who have given to perdition their own selves and those belonging to them on the day of judgement. Behold! Truly the wrongdoers are in a lasting penalty!" (Surat ash-Shura: 45)

Hell is full of hatred. Its hunger for disbelievers can never be satisfied. Despite an abundance of disbelievers, it still asks for more:

One day We will ask Hell, "Are you filled to the full?" It will say, "Are there any more (to come)?" (Surah Qaf: 30)

Allah describes the Hell in the Qur'an as follows:

Soon will I cast him into Saqar! And what will explain to you what Saqar is? Naught does it permit to endure, and naught does it leave alone, darkening and changing the colour of man! (Surat al-Muddaththir: 26-29)

An Endless Life Behind Locked Doors

As soon as disbelievers arrive in hell, the doors are locked behind them. Here, they see the most fearsome sights. They immediately understand that they will be "presented" to hell, the place where they will remain for eternity. The closed doors indicate that there will be no salvation. Allah describes the state of disbelievers as follows:

And (as for) those who disbelieve in Our signs, they are the people of the left hand. On them is fire closed over. (Surat al-Balad: 19-20)

The torment in the Qur'an is described as "a severe punishment" (Surah Ali-'Imran: 176), "a heavy doom" (Surah Ali-'Imran: 4), and "a painful chastisement" (Surah Ali-'Imran: 21). The descriptions of it are inadequate to give a full understanding of the punishment in hell. Being unable to resist even minor burns in the world, man cannot grasp being exposed to fire for all eternity. What is more, the pain that a fire gives in the world is incomparable to the severe torture of hell. No pain can be similar to that of hell:

> None punishes as He will punish on that day! None binds as He then will bind. (Surat al-Fajr: 25-26)

There is life in hell. Yet it is a life in which every moment is full of torture and anguish. Every type of physical, mental and psychological torment, various types of torture and disgrace rage in that life. To compare it to any distress in the world is impossible.

People in hell perceive pain through all five senses. Their eyes see disgusting and terrible images; their ears hear frightening screams, roars and cries; their noses fill with terrible and acrid smells; their tongues taste the most unbearable, vile tastes. They feel hell deep in their cells; this is a maddeningly severe pain that is difficult to imagine in this world. Their skin, their internal organs and their whole body are wracked and they writhe in pain.

The people of hell are very resistant to pain and they can never die. Hence, they can never save themselves from torture. In the Qur'an, this pain is described as follows: "What boldness (they show) for hell!" (Surat al-Baqarah: 175) Their skins are mended as they burn; the same torture continues for all eternity; the intensity of torture never decreases. Again, Allah says in the Qur'an: "Burn you therein. The same is it to you whether you bear it with patience, or not." (Surat at-Tur: 16)

No less than physical pain, mental pain is also severe in hell. People in hell regret deeply, fall into hopelessness, feel desperate and spend ages in despair. Every corner, every place in hell is designed to give mental suffering. The suffering is eternal; if it were to end after millions or billions years, even such a long-term possibility could arouse fervent hopes and remain a strong reason for happiness and joy. Yet, the eternity of torture will inspire a kind of hopelessness that cannot be compared to any similar feeling in this world.

According to the description of the Qur'an, hell is a place where extreme pain is experienced: disgusting smells; it is narrow, noisy, smoky and gloomy, injecting feelings of insecurity into human soul; fires burning deep in the heart; nasty food and drink; garments of fire and liquid pitch.

These are the basic characteristics of hell. There is a life going on in this terrible environment, however. The people of hell have sharp senses. They hear, talk and argue, and they try to escape from suffering. They burn in fire, become thirsty and hungry, and feel regret. They are tormented by feelings of guilt. What is more important, they want the pain to be relieved.

The people of hell live a life infinitely lower than the animals in this dirty and disgusting environment. The only nourishment they have is the fruits of the bitter thorn and the tree of zaqqum. Their drink, on the other hand, is blood and pus. Meanwhile, fire engulfs them everywhere. The anguish in hell is depicted as follows:

> Those who reject our Signs, We shall soon cast into hell. As often as their skins are roasted through, We shall change them for fresh skins that they may taste the penalty. For Allah is Exalted in Power, Wise. (Surat an-Nisa: 56)

With skin rent, flesh burned, and blood splattering all over, they are chained and whipped. Hands tied to their necks, they are cast into the core of hell. Angels of punishment, in the meantime, place those who are guilty in beds of fire, their covers also of fire. The coffins they are placed in are covered with fire.

Disbelievers constantly scream to be saved from such torments. And they often receive in reply only more humiliation and torture. They are left all alone in their anguish. Those who were known for their arrogance in the world now beg humbly for mercy. Furthermore, days in hell are not similar to days in the world, for how long is a minute of eternal suffering, how long a day, week, month or year of infinite unending pain?

These scenes will all come true. They are real. They are more real than our daily lives.

Those "who among men serve Allah, as it were, on the verge" (Surat al-Hajj: 11); those who say "the Fire shall not touch us but for a few numbered days" (Surah Ali-'Imran: 24); those who make notions such as money, status, and careers the main goals of their lives and accordingly neglect the good pleasure of Allah; those who alter the commands of Allah in accordance with their own wishes and desires; those who interpret the Qur'an according to their own interests; those who go astray from the right path – in brief – all disbelievers and hypocrites will abide in hell, except those whom Allah in His mercy forgives and rescues. This is the conclusive word of Allah and will certainly happen:

> If We had so willed, We could certainly have brought every soul its true guidance: but the word from Me will come true, "I will fill Hell with jinn and men all together." (Surat as-Sajdah: 13)

There is another fact about hell; these people are all specially created for hell, as the following verse suggests:

> Many are the jinn and men we have made for Hell: They have hearts wherewith they understand not, eyes wherewith they see not, and ears wherewith they hear not. They are like cattle – nay more misguided: for they are heedless (of warning). (Surat al-A'raf: 179)

Despite all the suffering they go through, there will not even be a single soul providing aid to the people of hell. No soul will be able to save them from it. Being abandoned will give them a bitter feeling of loneliness. "Therefore, he has not here today a true friend." (Surat al-Haqqah: 35) Around them, there will be only "the Angels of Punishment" who receive orders from Allah. These are extremely stern, merciless, and terrifying guards, bearing the sole responsibility of inflicting severe torture on the people of hell. The feeling of mercy is completely eradicated from the souls of these angels. Apart from their torments, they also have terrifying appearances, voices and gestures. The purpose of their existence is to take revenge upon those who rebel against Allah, and they exercise their responsibility with due care and attention. It is unlikely that they will provide "preferential treatment" to anybody.

This is, actually the real danger awaiting every soul on earth. Man, being rebellious and ungrateful to his Creator, and therefore committing the greatest wrong action, no doubt deserves such a recompense. Allah, therefore, warns man against it:

> O you who believe! Save yourselves and your families from a Fire whose fuel is men and stones, over which are (appointed) angels stern (and) severe, who flinch not (from executing) the commands they receive from Allah, but do (precisely) what they are commanded. (Surat at-Tahrim: 6)
>
> Let him beware! If he desist not, We will drag him by the forelock – a lying, sinful forelock! Then, let him call (for help) to his council (of comrades). We will call on the angels of punishment (to deal with him)! (Surat al-'Alaq: 15-18)

Pleas of Desperation and Hopelessness

The people of hell are in a hopeless state. The torture they undergo is extremely cruel and never-ending. Their only hope is to cry and beg for salvation. They see the People of paradise and beg for water and food. They try to repent and ask forgiveness of Allah. Yet, these are all in vain.

They beg the keepers of hell. They even want them be an intermediate between them and Allah and ask for mercy. Their pain is so unbearable that they want to be saved from it for even a single day:

> Those in the Fire will say to the keepers of hell: "Pray to your Lord to lighten us the penalty for a day (at least)!" They will say: "Did there not come to you your messengers with clear signs?" They will say, "Yes". They will reply, "Then pray (as you like)! But the prayer of those without faith is nothing but (futile wandering) in (mazes of) error!" (Surat al-Ghafir: 49-50)

Disbelievers further try to seek forgiveness, but they are strictly turned down:

> They will say:"Our Lord! Our misfortune overwhelmed us, and we became a people astray! Our Lord! Bring us out of this: if ever we return (to evil), then shall we be wrongdoers indeed!" He will say: "A part of My slaves there was, who used to pray 'our Lord! We believe; then forgive us, and have mercy upon us: for You are the Best of those who show mercy!' But you treated them with ridicule, so much so that (ridicule of) them made you forget My Message while you were laughing at them! I have rewarded them this Day

for their patience and constancy: they are indeed the ones that have achieved bliss." (Surat al-Muminun: 106-111)

This is actually the last address of Allah to the people of hell. His words "Be you driven into it (with ignominy)! And speak not to Me!" are conclusive. From then on, Allah never considers the people of hell. One would not even like to think about this situation.

While the people of hell burn in it, those who attain "happiness and salvation", in other words the believers, remain in paradise enjoying the benefit of endless favours. The suffering of the people of hell becomes more intense when they see and observe the life of believers in paradise. Indeed, while being subject to unbearable torture, they can "watch" the magnificent favours of paradise.

Believers, of whom disbelievers made fun in the world, now lead a full and happy life, living in glorious locations, magnificent houses with beautiful women, and tasting delicious food and drinks. The sight of the believers in peace and abundance further reinforces the humiliation of being in hell. These scenes add more pain and suffering to their grief.

> *(They will be) in gardens (of Delight): they will question each other, and (ask) of the wrongdoers: "What led you into Hell Fire?" They will say: "We were not of those who prayed; Nor were we of those who fed the indigent; But we used to talk vanities with vain talkers; And we used to deny the Day of Judgement, until there came to us (the Hour) that is certain." Then will no intercession of (any) intercessors profit them.*
> *(Surat al-Muddaththir: 40-48)*

The regret becomes deeper and deeper. Not having followed the commands of Allah in the world makes them feel profound remorse. They turn to the believers in paradise and try to speak to them. They beg for help and sympathy from them. Yet, these are vain efforts. The people of paradise also see them. Their glorious appearance and life make them feel more grateful to Allah. The exchange between the peoples of hell and paradise is as follows:

(They will be) in gardens (of Delight): they will question each other, and (ask) of the wrongdoers: "What led you into Hell Fire?"They will say: "We were not of those who prayed; Nor were we of those who fed the indigent; But we used to talk vanities with vain talkers; And we used to deny the day of judgement, until there came to us (the Hour) that is certain."Then will no intercession of (any) intercessors profit them. (Surat al-Muddaththir: 40-48)

An Important Reminder to Avoid Torment

In this chapter, we talked about two groups of people; those who have faith in Allah and those who reject His existence. We have also provided a general picture of hell, and one of paradise, based entirely on Qur'anic descriptions. Our purpose here is not to give some information on religion. This is to remind and warn disbelievers that the Hereafter will be a horrible place for them and theirs will be an awful doom.

After all that has been said, it is necessary to emphasise that man is, no doubt, free to make his choice. He can lead his life as he desires. No man has the right to force others to believe. However, as people who have faith in the existence of Allah and in His ultimate justice, we bear the responsibility of warning people against such a fearsome day. These people are surely unaware of the situation they are in and the kind of end awaiting them. Therefore, we feel a responsibility to warn them. Allah informs us about the state of these people:

> Which then is best? He that laid his foundation on fear of Allah and His good pleasure? Or he that laid his foundation on an undermined sand-cliff ready to crumble to pieces? And it crumbles to pieces with him, into the fire of Hell. And Allah guides not people that do wrong. (Surat at-Tawbah: 109)

Those who reject the commands of Allah in this world and, consciously or unconsciously, deny the existence of their Creator will have no salvation in the hereafter. Therefore, before losing any time, each one has to realise his situation in the presence of Allah and surrender to Him. Otherwise, he will regret it and face a fearsome end:

> Again and again will those who disbelieve wish that they had bowed (to Allah's will) in Islam. Leave them alone to enjoy (the good things of this life) and to please themselves: let (false) hope amuse them: soon will knowledge (undeceive them). (Surat al-Hijr: 2-3)

The way to avoid eternal punishment, win eternal bliss and attain the good pleasure of Allah is apparent:

Before it is too late, have true faith in Allah,

Spend your life doing good deeds to attain His good pleasure...

WARNING

The chapter you are about to read
reveals a crucial secret of your life.
You should read it very attentively
and thoroughly for it concerns a
subject that is liable to make
fundamental changes in your
outlook on the external world. The
subject of this chapter is not just a
point of view, a different approach,
or a traditional or philosophical
thought: it is a fact which
everyone, believing or unbelieving,
must admit and which is also
proven by science today.

The Real Essence
of Matter

People who conscientiously and wisely contemplate their surroundings realise that everything in the universe – both animate and inanimate – must have been created. The question is "Who is the Creator of all these things?"

It is evident that **"the fact of creation"**, which reveals itself in every aspect of the universe, cannot be an outcome of the universe itself. For example, a bug cannot have created itself. The solar system cannot have created or organised itself. Neither plants, humans, bacteria, erythrocytes (red-blood corpuscles), nor butterflies can have created themselves. Also the possibility that all these could have originated "by chance" is not even imaginable.

We therefore arrive at the following conclusion: Everything that we see has been created, but nothing we see can themselves be "creators". The Creator is different from and superior to all that we see with our eyes, a superior power that is invisible but whose existence and attributes are revealed in everything that exists.

This is the point at which those who deny the existence of Allah demur. These people are conditioned not to believe in His existence unless they see Him with their eyes. These people, who disregard the fact of **"creation"**, are forced to ignore the actuality of "creation" manifest throughout the universe and try to prove that the universe and the living things in it have not been created. Evolutionary theory is an essential example of their vain endeavours to this end.

The basic mistake of those who deny Allah is shared by many people who do not really deny the existence of Allah but have a wrong perception of Him. They do not deny creation but have superstitious beliefs about "where" Allah is. Most of them think that Allah is up in the "sky". They tacitly imagine that Allah is behind a very distant planet and interferes with "worldly affairs" once in a while, or perhaps does not intervene at all. They imagine that He created the universe and then left it to itself leaving people to determine their fates for themselves.

Still others have heard that it is written in the Qur'an that Allah is "everywhere" but they cannot conceive what exactly this means. They think that Allah surrounds everything like radio waves or like an invisible, intangible gas.

However, this and other beliefs that are unable to make clear **"where" Allah is** (and maybe because of that deny Him) are all based on a common mistake. They are prejudiced without any grounds for it and so are then moved to wrong opinions of Allah. What is this prejudice?

This prejudice is about the nature and characteristics of matter. We are so conditioned in our suppositions about the existence of matter that we never think whether it does exist or not or whether it is only a shadow. Modern science demolishes this prejudice and discloses a very important and revealing reality. In the following pages, we will try to clarify this great reality to which the Qur'an points.

The World of Electrical Signals

All the information that we have about the world in which we live is conveyed to us by our five senses. The world we know of consists of what our eyes see, our hands feel, our noses smell, our tongues taste, and our ears hear. We never think that the "external" world could be anything other than that which our senses present to us, as we have been dependent on only those senses since birth.

Modern research in many different fields of science points to a very different understanding and creates serious doubt about our senses and the world that we perceive with them.

The starting-point of this approach is that the notion of an "external world" shaped in our brain is only a response created in our brain by electrical signals. The redness of apples, the hardness of wood and, moreover, your mother, father, family, and everything that you own, your house, job, and the lines of this book, are comprised only of electrical signals.

Frederick Vester explains the point that science has reached on this subject:

> Statements of some scientists posing that **"man is an image**, everything experienced is temporary and deceptive, and **this universe is a shadow"**, seems to be proven by science in our day.[14]

The famous philosopher, George Berkeley commented on the subject as follows:

> We believe in the existence of objects just because we see and touch them, and they are reflected to us by our perceptions. However, our perceptions are only ideas in our mind. Thus, objects we captivate by perceptions are nothing but ideas, and these ideas are essentially in nowhere but our mind... Since all these exist only in the mind, then it means that **we are beguiled by deceptions when we imagine the universe and things to have an existence outside the mind.** So, none of the surrounding things have an existence out of our mind.[15]

In order to clarify the subject, let us consider our sense of sight, which provides us with the most extensive information about the external world.

How Do We See, Hear, and Taste?

The act of seeing is realised progressively. Light clusters (photons) travel from the object to the eye and pass through the lens at the front of the eye where they are refracted and fall upside-down on the retina at the back of the eye. Here, impinging light is turned into electrical signals that are transmitted by neurons to a tiny spot called the centre of vision in the back of the brain. This electrical signal is perceived as an image in this centre in the brain after a series of processes. The act of seeing actually takes place in this tiny spot in the posterior part of the brain, which is **pitch-dark and completely insulated from light**.

Now, let us reconsider this seemingly ordinary and unremarkable process. When we say, "we see", we are in fact seeing the effects of impulses reaching our eyes and induced in our brain, after they are transformed into electrical signals. That is, **when we say, "we see", we are actually observing electrical signals in our mind**.

All the images we view in our lives are formed in our centre of vision, which only comprises a few cubic centimetres of the volume of the brain. Both the book you are now reading and the boundless landscape you see when you gaze at the horizon fit into this tiny space. Another point that has to be kept in mind is that, as we have noted before, the brain is insulated from light; its inside is absolutely dark. The brain has no contact with light itself.

We can explain this interesting situation with an example. Let us suppose that in front of us there is a burning candle. We can sit opposite this candle and watch it at length. However, during this period, our brain never has any direct contact with the original light of the candle. Even as we see the light of the candle, the inside of our brain is completely dark. We watch a colourful and bright world inside our dark brain.

R. L. Gregory gives the following explanation about the miraculous aspects of seeing, something that we take so much for granted:

> We are so familiar with seeing, that it takes a leap of imagination to realise that there are problems to be solved. But consider it. We are given tiny dis-

Stimulations coming from an object are converted into electrical signals and cause effects in the brain. When we "see", we in fact view the effects of these electrical signals in our mind.

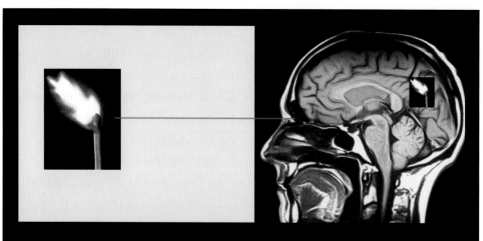

Even at the moment when we feel the light and heat of a fire, the inside of our brain is pitch dark and its temperature never changes.

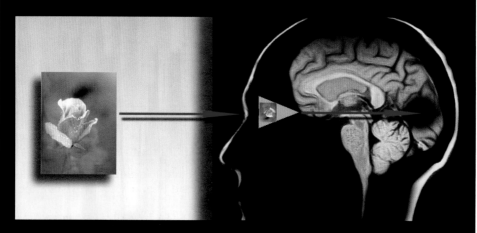

Bundles of light coming from an object falls upside-down on the retina. Here, the image is converted into electrical signals and transmitted to the centre of vision at the back of the brain. Since the brain is insulated from light, it is impossible for light to reach the centre of vision. This means that we view a vast world of light and depth in a tiny spot that is insulated from light.

torted upside-down images in the eyes, and we see separate solid objects in surrounding space. From the patterns of simulation on the retinas we perceive the world of objects, and **this is nothing short of a miracle.**[16]

The same situation applies to all our other senses. Sound, touch, taste and smell are all transmitted to the brain as electrical signals and are perceived in the relevant centres in the brain.

The sense of hearing works in a similar manner to that of sight. The outer ear picks up sounds by the auricle and directs them to the middle ear. The middle ear transmits the sound vibrations to the inner ear and intensifies them. The inner ear translates the vibrations into electrical signals, which it sends into the brain. Just as with the eye, the act of hearing finally takes place in the centre of hearing in the brain. The brain is insulated from sound just as it is from light. Therefore, no matter how noisy it is outside, the inside of the brain is completely silent.

Nevertheless, even the subtlest sounds are perceived in the brain. This is so precise that the ear of a healthy person hears everything without any atmospheric noise or interference. In your brain, which is insulated from sound, you listen to the symphonies of an orchestra, hear all the noises of a crowded place, and perceive all the sounds within a wide frequency range, from the rustling of a leaf to the roar of a jet plane. However, if the sound level in your brain were to be measured by a sensitive device at that moment, it would be seen that a complete silence is prevailing there.

Our perception of odour is formed in a similar way. Volatile molecules emitted by things such as vanilla or a rose reach the receptors in the delicate hairs in the epithelium region of the nose and become involved in an interaction. This interaction is transmitted to the brain as electrical signals and perceived as smell. Everything that we smell, be it pleasant or unpleasant, is nothing but the brain's perception of the interactions of volatile mol-

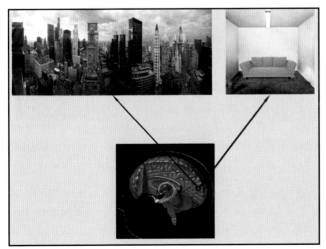

All we see in our lives is formed in a part of our brain called the "vision centre" which lies at the back of our brain, and which occupies only a few cubic centimetres. Both the book you are now reading and the boundless landscape you see when you gaze at the horizon fit into this tiny space. Therefore, we see objects not in their actual sizes existing outside, but in the sizes perceived by our brain.

ecules after they have been transformed into electrical signals. You perceive the scent of a perfume, a flower, a food that you like, the sea, or other odours you like or dislike, in your brain. The molecules themselves never reach the brain. Just as with sound and vision, what reach your brain simply electrical signals. In other words, all the odours that you have assumed – since you were born – to belong to external objects are just electrical signals that you feel through your sense organs.

Similarly, there are four different types of chemical receptors in the front part of a human's tongue. These pertain to the four tastes: salty, sweet, sour, and bitter. Our taste receptors transform these perceptions into electrical signals through a chain of chemical processes and transmit them to the brain. These signals are perceived as taste by the brain. The taste you experience when you eat a chocolate bar or a fruit that you like is the interpretation of electrical signals by the brain. You can never reach the object in the external world; you can never see, smell or taste the chocolate itself. For instance, if the taste nerves that travel to the brain are cut, the taste of things you eat will not reach your brain; you will completely lose your sense of taste.

At this point, we come across another fact: We can never be sure that what we experience when we taste a food and what another person experiences when he tastes the same food, or what we perceive when we hear a voice and what another person perceives when he hears the same voice are the same. Lincoln Barnett says that no one can know whether another person perceives the colour red or hears the C note the in same way as does he himself.[17]

Our sense of touch is no different from the others. When we touch an object, all information that will help us recognise the external world and objects are transmitted to the brain by the sense nerves on the skin. The feeling of touch is formed in our brain. Contrary to general belief, the place where we perceive the sense of touch is not at our finger-tips or on our skins but at the centre of touch perception in our brains. Because of the brain's interpretation of electrical stimuli coming to it from objects, we experience those objects differently such as that they are hard or soft, hot or cold. We derive all the details that help us recognise an object from these stimuli. Concerning this, the thoughts of two famous philosophers, B. Russell and L. Wittgenstein, are as follows:

> For instance, whether a lemon truly exists or not and how it came to exist cannot be questioned and investigated. A lemon consists merely of a taste sensed by the tongue, an odour sensed by the nose, a colour and shape sensed by the eye; and only these features of it can be subject to examination and assessment. Science can never know the physical world.[18]

It is impossible for us to reach the physical world. All objects around us are a collection of perceptions such as seeing, hearing, and touching. By processing the data in the centre of vision and in other sensory centres, our brains, throughout our lives, **do not confront the "original" of the matter existing outside us but rather the copy formed inside our brain.** It is at this point that we are misled by assuming these copies are instances of real matter outside us.

"The External World" Inside Our Brain

From the physical facts described so far, we may conclude the following. Everything we see, touch, hear, and perceive as "matter", "the world" or "the universe" is only electrical signals occurring in our brain.

Someone eating a fruit does not confront the actual fruit but its perception in the brain. The object considered by the person a "fruit" actually consists of electrical impressions of the shape, taste, smell, and texture of the fruit in the brain. If the sight nerves travelling to the brain were to be severed suddenly, the image of the fruit would suddenly disappear. A disconnection in the nerve travelling from the sensors in the nose to the brain would completely interrupt the sense of smell. Put simply, the fruit is nothing but the brain's interpretation of electrical signals.

Another point to be considered is **the sense of distance**. Distance, for example the distance between you and this book, is only a feeling of space formed in your brain. Objects that seem to be distant in one person's view also exist in the brain. For instance, someone who watches the stars in the sky assumes that they are millions of light-years away from him. Yet, what

he "sees" are really the stars inside himself, in his centre of vision. While you read these lines, you are, in truth, not inside the room you assume yourself to be in; on the contrary, the room is inside you. Your seeing your body makes you think that you are inside it. **However, you must remember that your body, too, is an image formed inside your brain.**

The same applies to all your other perceptions. For instance, when you think that you hear the sound of the television in the next room, you are actually experiencing the sound inside your brain. You can prove neither that a room exists next to yours, nor that a sound comes from the television in that room. Both the sound you think to be coming from metres away and the conversation of a person right next to you are perceived in a centre of hearing a few centimetres square in your brain. Apart from in this centre of perception, no concept such as right, left, front or behind exists. That is, sound does not come to you from the right, from the left or from the air; **there is no direction from which sound comes.**

The smells that you perceive are like that too; none of them reaches you from a great distance. You suppose that the end-effects formed in your centre of smell are the smell of the objects in the external world. However, just as the image of a rose is in your centre of vision, so the smell of the rose is in your centre of smell; there is neither a rose nor an odour pertaining to it in the external world.

The "external world" presented to us by our perceptions is merely a collection of electrical signals reaching our brains. Throughout our lives, our brains process these signals and we live without recognising that we are mistaken in assuming that these are the original versions of things existing in the "external world". We are misled because we can never reach the matters themselves by means of our senses.

Moreover, again our brains interpret and attribute meaning to signals that we assume to be the "external world". For example, let us consider the sense of hearing. Our brains transform the sound waves in the "external world" into a symphony. That is to say, music is also a perception created by our brains. In the same manner, when we see colours, what reach our eyes are merely electrical signals of **different wavelengths**. Again our brains transform these signals into colours. **There are no colours in the "external world".** Neither is the apple red nor is the sky blue nor the trees green. They are as they are just because we perceive them to be so. **The "external world" depends entirely on the perceiver.**

BEYOND REALITY
Is the universe really a frolic of primal information and matter just a mirage?

Even the slightest defect in the retina of the eye causes colour blindness. Some people perceive blue as green, some red as blue, and some perceive all colours as different tones of grey. At this point, it does not matter whether the object externally is coloured or not.

The prominent thinker Berkeley also addressed this fact:

> At the beginning, it was believed that **colours, odours**, etc., "really exist", but subsequently such views were renounced, and it was seen that

The findings of modern physics show that the universe is a collection of perceptions. The following question appears on the cover of the well-known American science magazine New Scientist, which dealt with this matter in its 30 January 1999 issue: "Beyond Reality: Is the Universe Really a Frolic of Primal Information and Matter Just a Mirage?"

they only exist in dependence on our sensations.[19]

In conclusion, the reason we see objects coloured is not because they are coloured or because they have an independent material existence outside ourselves. The truth of the matter is rather that **all the qualities we ascribe to objects are inside us and not in the "external world".**

So what remains of the "external world"?

Is the Existence of the "External World" Indispensable?

So far, we have been speaking repeatedly of an "external world" and a world of perceptions formed in our brains, the latter of which is what we see. However, since we can never actually reach the "external world", how can we be sure that such a world really exists?

Actually we cannot. Since each object is only a collection of perceptions and those perceptions exist only in the mind, it is more accurate to say that **the only world that really exists is the world of perceptions.** The only world we know of is the world that exists in our mind: the one that is designed, recorded, and made vivid there; the one, in short, that is created within our mind. This is the only world of which we can be sure.

We can never prove that the perceptions we observe in our brain have material correlates. Those perceptions could conceivably be coming from an "artificial" source.

It is possible to observe this. False stimuli can produce an entirely imaginary "material world" in our brain. For example, let us imagine a very developed recording instrument in which all kinds of electrical signals could be recorded. First, let us transmit all the data related to a setting (including body image) to this instrument by transforming them into electrical signals. Second, let us imagine that the brain could survive apart from the body. Finally, let us connect the recording instrument to the brain with electrodes that will function as nerves and send the pre-recorded data to the brain. In this state, you would experience yourself living in this artificially created setting. For instance, you could easily believe that you are driving fast on a highway. It might never become possible to understand that you consist of nothing but your brain. This is because what is needed to form a world within your brain is not the existence of a real world but rather the stimuli. It is perfectly possible that these stimuli could be coming from an artificial source, such as a tape-recorder.

In that connection, distinguished philosopher Bertrand Russell wrote:

> As to the sense of touch when we press the table with our fingers, that is an electric disturbance on the electrons and protons of our fingertips, produced, according to modern physics, by the proximity of the electrons and protons in the table. **If the same disturbance in our finger-tips arose in any other way, we should have the sensations, in spite of there being no table.**[20]

It is indeed very easy for us to be deceived into believing perceptions, without any material correlates, to be real. We often experience this feeling in our dreams, in which we experience events, see people, objects and settings that seem completely real. However, they are all nothing but mere perceptions. There is no basic difference between the dream and the "real world"; both of them are experienced in the brain.

Who Is the Perceiver?

As we have related so far, there is no doubt that the world we think we inhabit and that we call the "external world" is perceived inside our brain. However, here arises the question of primary importance. If all physical events that we know are intrinsically perceptions, what about our brain? Since our brains are a part of the physical world just like our arms, legs, or any other objects, it also must be a perception just like all other objects.

An example about dreams will illuminate the subject further. Let us think that we see the dream within our brain in accordance with what has been said so far. In the dream, we will have an imaginary body, an imaginary arm, an imaginary eye, and an imaginary brain. If during our dream, we were asked, "where do you see?" we would answer "I see in my brain". Yet, actually there is not any brain to talk about, but an imaginary head and an imaginary brain. The seer of the images is not the imaginary brain in the dream, but a "being" that is far "superior" to it.

We know that there is no physical distinction between the setting of a dream and the setting we call real life. So when we are asked in the setting we call real life the above question "where do you see", it would be just as meaningless to answer "in my brain" as in the example above. In both conditions, the entity that sees and perceives is not the brain, which is after all only a hunk of meat.

When we analyse the brain, we see that there is nothing in it but lipid and protein molecules, which also exist in other living organisms. This means that within the piece of meat we call our "brain", there is nothing to observe the images, to constitute consciousness, or to create the being we call "myself".

R. L. Gregory refers to a mistake people make in relation to the perception of images in the brain:

> There is a temptation, which must be avoided, to say that the eyes produce pictures in the brain. A picture in the brain suggests the need of some kind of internal eye to see it – but this would need a further eye to see its picture... and so on in an endless regress of eyes and pictures. This is absurd.[21]

This is the very point that puts materialists, who do not hold anything but matter to be true, in a quandary: to whom belongs "the eye inside" that sees, that perceives what it sees and reacts?

Karl Pribram also focused on this important question, about who the perceiver is, in the world of science and philosophy:

> Philosophers since the Greeks have speculated about the "ghost" in the machine, the "little man inside the little man" and so on. **Where is the I – the entity that uses the brain? Who does the actual knowing?** Or, as Saint Francis of Assisi once put it, "What we are looking for is what is looking."[22]

Now, think of this: The book in your hand, the room you are in, in brief, all the images in front of you are seen inside your brain. Is it the atoms that see these images? Blind, deaf, unconscious atoms? Why did some atoms acquire this quality whereas some did not? Do our acts of thinking, comprehending, remembering, being delighted, being unhappy, and everything else consist of the electrochemical reactions between these atoms?

When we ponder these questions, we see that there is no sense in looking for will in atoms. It is clear that the being that sees, hears, and feels is a supra-material being. This being is "alive" and it is neither matter nor an

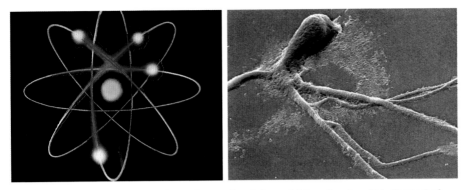

The brain is a collection of cells made up of protein and fat molecules. It is formed of nerve cells called neurons. There is no power in this piece of meat to observe images, to constitute consciousness, or to create the being we call "myself".

image of matter. This being associates with the perceptions in front of it by using the image of our body.

This being is the "soul".

The aggregate of perceptions we call the "material world" is a dream observed by this soul. Just as the bodies we possess and the material world we see in our dreams have no reality, the universe we occupy and the bodies we possess also have no material reality.

The real being is the soul. Matter consists merely of perceptions viewed by the soul. The intelligent beings that write and read these lines are not each a heap of atoms and molecules and the chemical reactions between them, but a "soul".

The Real Absolute Being

All these facts bring us face to face with a very significant question. If the thing we acknowledge to be the material world is merely comprised of perceptions seen by our soul, then what is the source of these perceptions?

In answering this question, we must consider the following: matter does not have a self-governing existence by itself. Since matter is a perception, it is something "artificial". That is, this perception must have been caused by another power, which means that it must have been created. Moreover, this creation must be continuous. If there were not a continuous and consistent creation, then what we call matter would disappear and be lost. This may be likened to a television on which a picture is displayed as long as the signal continues to be broadcast. So, who makes our soul see the stars, the earth, plants, people, our bodies and all else that we see?

It is very evident that there is a Creator, Who has created the entire material universe, that is, the sum of perceptions, and continues His creation ceaselessly. Since this Creator displays such a magnificent creation, He surely has eternal power and might.

This Creator introduces Himself to us. He has revealed a Book and through this Book has described Himself, the universe and the reason of our existence to us.

This Creator is Allah and the name of His Book is the Qur'an.

The facts that the heavens and the earth, that is, the universe is not stable, that their presence is only made possible by Allah's creating them and that they will disappear when He ends this creation, are all explained in a verse as follows:

> It is Allah Who sustains the heavens and the earth, lest they cease (to function): and if they should fail, there is none - not one - can sustain them thereafter: Verily He is Most Forbearing, Oft-Forgiving. (Surat al-Fatir: 41)

As we mentioned at the beginning, some people have no genuine understanding of Allah and so they imagine Him as a being present somewhere in the heavens and not really intervening in worldly affairs. The basis of this logic actually lies in the thought that the universe is an assembly of matter and Allah is "outside" this material world, in a far away place. In some false religions, belief in Allah is limited to this understanding.

However, as we have considered so far, matter is composed only of sensations. And the only real absolute being is Allah. That means that **only Allah is; all things except Him are shadow beings.** Consequently, it is impossible to conceive of Allah as separate and outside of this whole mass of matter. **Allah is surely "everywhere" and encompasses all.** This reality is explained in the Qur'an as follows;

> Allah! There is no god but He, the Living, the Self-subsisting, Eternal. No slumber can seize Him nor sleep. His are all things in the heavens and on earth. Who is there can intercede in His presence except as He permits? He knows what (appears to His creatures as) before or after or behind them. Nor

shall they compass aught of His knowledge except as He wills. **His Throne extends over the heavens and the earth,** and He feels no fatigue in guarding and preserving them for He is the Most High, the Supreme (in glory). (Surat al-Baqarah: 255)

That Allah is not bound by space and that He encompasses everything roundabout is stated in another verse as follows:

To Allah belong the east and the West: **Whithersoever you turn, there is the Face of Allah**. For Allah is all-pervading, all-knowing. (Surat al-Baqarah: 115)

Since material beings are each a perception, they cannot see Allah; but Allah sees the matter He created in all its forms. In the Qur'an, this is stated thus: **"No vision can grasp Him, but His grasp is over all vision."** (Surat al-An'am: 103)

That is, we cannot grasp Allah's being with our eyes, but Allah has thoroughly encompassed our inside, outside, looks and thoughts. We cannot utter any word but with His knowledge, nor can we even take a breath.

While we watch these sensory perceptions in the course of our lives, the closest being to us is not any one of these sensations, but Allah Himself. The secret of the following verse in the Qur'an is concealed in this reality: "It is We Who created man, and We know what dark suggestions his soul makes to him: for **We are nearer to him than (his) jugular vein.**" (Surah Qaf: 16) When a person thinks that his body is only made up of "matter", he cannot comprehend this important fact. If he takes his brain to be "himself", then the place that he accepts to be the outside is 20-30 cm away from him. However, when he understands that there is nothing such as matter, and that everything is imagination, notions such as outside, inside, far or near lose meaning. **Allah has encompassed him and He is "infinitely close" to him.**

Allah informs men that He is **"infinitely close"** to them with the verse "When My servants ask you concerning Me, **I am indeed close (to them)."** (Surat al-Baqarah: 186). Another verse relates the

Why is it not then that when it (soul) comes up to the throat, and you at that time look on, We are nearer to it than you, but you see not. (Surat al-Waqia, 83-85)

If one ponders deeply on all that is said here, one will soon realise this amazing, extraordinary situation by oneself: that all the events in the world are but mere imagination...

same fact: "We told you that **your Lord encompasses mankind round about.**" (Surat al-Isra, 60).

Man is misled in thinking that the being closest to him is himself. Allah, in truth, is even closer to us than ourselves. He has called our attention to this point in the verse "Why is it not then that when it (soul) comes up to the throat, and you at that time look on, **We are nearer to him than you,** but you see not." (Surat al-Waqi'ah: 83-85). As we are told in the verse, people live unaware of this phenomenal fact because they do not see it with their eyes.

On the other hand, it is impossible for man, who is nothing but a shadow being, to have power and will independent of Allah. The verse "But

Allah has created you and what you do!" (Surat as-Saffat: 96) shows that everything we experience takes place under Allah's control. In the Qur'an, this reality is stated in the verse "**You did not throw, when you threw, it was Allah who threw**" (Surat al-Anfal, 17) whereby it is emphasised that no act is independent of Allah. Since the human being is a shadow being, he himself does not perform the act of throwing. However, Allah gives this shadow being the feeling of self. In reality, Allah performs all acts. If someone takes the acts he does as his own, he evidently means to deceive himself.

This is the reality. A person may not want to concede this and may think of himself as a being independent of Allah; but this does not change a thing. Of course his unwise denial is again within Allah's will and wish.

Everything That You Possess Is Intrinsically Illusory

As may be seen clearly, it is a logical scientific fact that the "external world" has no material reality and that it is a collection of images perpetually presented to our soul by Allah. Nevertheless, people usually do not include, or rather do not want to include, everything in the concept of the "external world".

Think about this issue sincerely and boldly. You will realise that your house, furniture, car – which is perhaps recently bought, office, jewellery, bank account, wardrobe, spouse, children, colleagues, and everything else that you possess are in fact included in this imaginary external world projected to you. Everything you see, hear, or smell – in short – perceive with your five senses around you is a part of this "imaginary world": the voice of your favourite singer, the hardness of the chair you sit on, a perfume whose smell you like, the sun that keeps you warm, a flower with beautiful colours, a bird flying in front of your window, a speedboat moving swiftly on the water, your fertile garden, the computer you use at your job, or your hi-fi that has the most advanced technology in the world...

This is the reality, because the world is only a collection of images created to test man. People are tested all through their limited lives with perceptions having no reality. These perceptions are intentionally presented as appealing and attractive. This fact is mentioned in the Qur'an:

> Fair in the eyes of people is the love of things they covet: Women and sons; heaped-up hoards of gold and silver; horses branded (for blood and excellence); and (wealth of) cattle and well-tilled land. Such are the possessions of this world's life; but in nearness to Allah is the best of the goals (to return to). (Surat Ali 'Imran: 14)

Most people cast their religion away for the lure of property, wealth, heaped-up hoards of gold and silver, dollars, jewellery, bank accounts, credit cards, wardrobes full of clothes, last-model cars, in short, all the forms of prosperity that they either possess or strive to possess. They concentrate only on this world while forgetting the hereafter. They are deceived by the "fair and alluring" face of the life of this world, and fail to keep up prayer, give charity to the poor, and perform worship that will make them prosper in the hereafter. They say instead, "I have things to do", "I have ideals", "I have responsibilities", "I do not have enough time", "I have things to complete" and "I will do it in the future". They consume their lives trying to prosper only in this world. In the verse, **"They know but the outer (things) in the life of this world: but of the End of things they are heedless"** (Surat ar-Rum: 7), this misconception is described.

The fact we describe in this chapter, namely that everything is an image, is very important for its implications that render all lusts and boundaries meaningless. The verification of this fact makes it clear that everything people possess or toil to possess – wealth acquired with greed, children of whom they boast, spouses whom they consider closest to them, friends, their dearest bodies, the social status which they believe to be a superiority, the schools they have attended, the holidays on which they have been – is nothing but mere illusion. Therefore, all the effort, the time spent, and the greed, prove unavailing.

This is why some people unwittingly make fools of themselves when they boast of their wealth and properties or of their "yachts, helicopters, factories, holdings, manors and lands" as if they really exist. Those well-to-do people who ostentatiously sail in their yachts, show off their cars, keep talking about their wealth, suppose that their posts rank them higher than everyone else and keep thinking that they are successful because of all this, should actually think what kind of a state they will find themselves in once they realise that success is nothing but an illusion.

These scenes are seen many times in dreams as well. In their dreams, they also have houses, fast cars, extremely precious jewels, rolls of dollars, and loads of gold and silver. In their dreams, they are also positioned in high ranks, own factories with thousands of workers, possess power to rule over many people, and dress in clothes that make everyone admire them. Just as someone who, on waking, boasted about his possessions in his dreams would be ridiculed, he is sure to be equally ridiculed for boasting of images he sees in this world. Both what he sees in his dreams and in this world are mere images in his mind.

Similarly, the way people react to events they experience in the world will make them feel ashamed when they realise the reality. Those who fiercely fight with each other, rave furiously, swindle, take bribes, commit forgery, lie, covetously withhold their money, do wrong to people, beat and curse others, rage aggressively, are full of passion for office and rank, are envious, and show off, will be disgraced when they realise that they have done all of this in a dream.

Since Allah creates all these images, the Ultimate Owner of everything is Allah alone. This fact is stressed in the Qur'an:

> But to Allah belong all things in the heavens and on earth: And He it is that encompasses all things. (Surat an-Nisa: 126)

It is great foolishness to cast religion away for the sake of imaginary passions and thus lose the eternal life.

At this stage, one point should be understood. It is not said here that "the possessions, wealth, children, spouses, friends, rank you have with which you are being stingy will vanish sooner or later, and therefore they do not have any meaning", but that "all the possessions you seem to have do not exist, but they are merely dreams composed of images which Allah shows you to test you". As you see, there is a big difference between the two statements.

Although one does not want to acknowledge this right away and would rather deceive oneself by assuming everything one has truly exists, one is finally to die and in the hereafter everything will be clear when we are recreated. On that day **"sharp is one's sight"** (Surah Qaf: 22) and we will see everything much more clearly. However, if we have spent our lives chasing after imaginary aims, we are going to wish we had never lived this life and say "Ah! Would that (Death) had made an end of me! Of no profit to me has been my wealth! My power has perished from me!" (Surat al-Haqqah: 27-29)

What a wise man should do, on the other hand, is to try to understand the greatest reality of the universe here in this world, while he still has time. Otherwise, he will spend all his life running after dreams and face a grievous penalty at the end. In the Qur'an, the final state of those people who run after illusions (or mirages) in this world and forget their Creator, is stated as follows:

> **But the unbelievers, their deeds are like a mirage in sandy deserts,** which the man parched with thirst mistakes for water; until when he comes up to it, he finds it to be nothing: But he finds Allah (ever) with him, and Allah will pay him his account: and Allah is swift in taking account. (Surat an-Nur: 39)

Logical Defects of the Materialists

From the beginning of this chapter, it is clearly stated that matter does not have absolute being, as materialists claim, but is rather a collection of sense impressions created by Allah. Materialists resist this evident reality, which destroys their philosophy, in an extremely dogmatic manner and bring forward baseless anti-theses.

For example, one of the biggest advocates of materialist philosophy in the 20th century, an ardent Marxist, **George Politzer**, gave the **"bus example"** as the "greatest evidence" for the existence of matter. According to Politzer, philosophers who think that matter is only a perception also run away when they see a bus about to run them over and this is the proof of the physical existence of matter.[23]

When another famous materialist, Johnson, was told that matter is a collection of perceptions, he tried to "prove" the physical existence of stones by giving them a kick.[24]

A similar example is given by **Friedrich Engels**, the mentor of Politzer and founder, along with Marx, of dialectical materialism. He wrote, **"if the cakes we eat were mere perceptions, they would not stop our hunger"**.[25]

There are similar examples and some outrageous sentences such as **"you understand the existence of matter when you are slapped in the face"** in the books of famous materialists such as **Marx**, **Engels**, **Lenin**, and others.

The disorder in comprehension that gives way to these examples of the materialists is their interpreting the explanation of "matter is a perception" as "matter is a trick of light". They think that perception is limited to sight and that other faculties like touch have physical correlates. A bus knocking down a man makes them say "look, it crashed, therefore it is not a perception". They do not understand that all perceptions experienced during a bus crash, such as hardness, collision, and pain, are also formed in the brain.

The Example of Dreams

The best example to explain this reality is the dream. A person can experience very realistic events in dream. He can roll down the stairs and break his leg, have a serious car accident, become stuck under a bus, or eat a cake and be satiated. Similar events to those experienced in our daily lives are also experienced in dreams with the same persuasive sense of their reality, and arousing the same feelings in us.

A person who dreams that he is knocked down by a bus can open his eyes in a hospital again in his dream and understand that he is disabled, but it is all a dream. He can also dream that he dies in a car crash, angels of death take his soul, and his life in the hereafter begins. (This latter event is experienced in the same manner in this life, which, just like the dream, is a perception.)

This person perceives very sharply the images, sounds, feelings of solid-

For you, reality is all that can be touched with the hand and seen with the eye. In your dreams you can also "touch with your hand and see with your eye", but in reality, then you have neither hand nor eye, nor is there anything that can be touched or seen. There is no material reality that makes these things happen except your brain. You are simply being deceived.

What is it that separates real life and dreams from one another? Ultimately, both forms of living are brought into being within the brain. If we are able to live easily in an unreal world during our dreams, the same can equally be true for the world we live in while awake. When we wake up from a dream, there is no logical reason not to think that we have entered a longer dream called "real life". The reason we consider our dream a fancy and the world 'real' is only a product of our habits and prejudices. This suggests that we may well be awoken from the life on earth, which we think we are living right now, just as we are awoken from a dream.

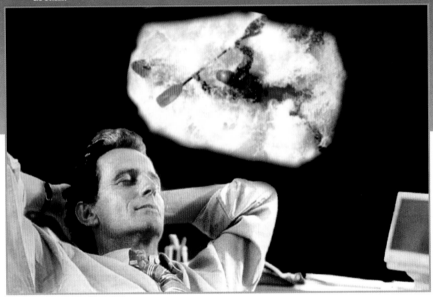

ity, light, colours, and all other feelings pertaining to the event he experiences in his dream. The perceptions he perceives in his dream are as natural as the ones in "real" life. The cake he eats in his dream satiates him although it is a mere dream-sense perception, because being satiated is also a dream-sense perception. However, in reality, this person is lying in his bed at that moment. There are no stairs, traffic, or buses to consider.

The dreaming person experiences and sees perceptions and feelings that do not exist in the external world. The fact that in our dreams, we experience, see, and feel events with no physical correlates in the "external world" very clearly reveals that the "external world" of our waking lives also consists absolutely of mere perceptions.

Those who believe in materialist philosophy, particularly **Marxists**, are enraged when they are told about this reality, the essence of matter. They quote examples from the superficial reasoning of **Marx**, **Engels**, or **Lenin** and make emotional declarations.

However, these persons must think that they can also make these declarations in their dreams. In their dreams, they can also read "Das Kapital", participate in meetings, fight with the police, be hit on the head, and feel the pain of their wounds. When asked in their dreams, they will think that what they experience in their dreams also consists of "absolute matter", just as they assume the things they see when they are awake are "absolute matter". However, whether it is in their dreams or in their daily lives, all that they see, experience, or feel consists only of perceptions.

The Example of Connecting the Nerves in Parallel

Let us consider the car crash example given by Politzer in which he talked of someone crushed by a car. If the crushed person's nerves travelling from his five senses to his brain, were connected to another person's, take Politzer's brain, with a parallel connection, at the moment the bus hit that person, it would also hit Politzer sitting at home at the same time. All the feelings experienced by that person having the accident would be experienced by Politzer, just like the same song listened to from two different loudspeakers connected to the same tape recorder. Politzer would feel, see, and experience the braking of the bus, the touch of the bus on his body, the images of a broken arm and blood, fractures, images of his entering the operation room, the hardness of the plaster cast, and the feebleness of his arm.

Every other person connected to the man's nerves in parallel would experience the accident from beginning to end just like Politzer. If the man in the accident fell into a coma, they would all fall into a coma. Moreover, if all the perceptions pertaining to the car accident were recorded in a device and if all these perceptions were transmitted to a person repeatedly, the bus would knock this person down many times.

So, which one of the buses hitting those people is real? The materialist philosophy has no consistent answer to this question. The right answer is that they all experience the car accident in all its details in their own minds.

The same principle applies to the cake and stone examples. If the nerves of the sense organs of Engels, who felt the satiety and fullness of the cake in his stomach after eating a cake, were connected to a second person's brain in parallel, that person would also feel full when Engels ate the cake and was satiated. If the nerves of Johnson, who felt pain in his foot when he delivered a sound kick to a stone, were connected to a second person in parallel, that person would feel the same pain.

So, which cake or which stone is the real one? The materialist philosophy again falls short of giving a consistent answer to this question. The correct and consistent answer is this: both Engels and the second person have eaten the cake in their minds and are satiated; both Johnson and the second person have fully experienced the moment of striking the stone in their minds.

Let us make a change in the example we gave about Politzer: let us connect the nerves of the man hit by the bus to Politzer's brain, and the nerves of Politzer sitting in his house to the brain of the man who is hit by the bus. In this case, Politzer will think that a bus has hit him although he is sitting in his house. The man actually hit by the bus will never feel the impact of the accident and think that he is sitting in Politzer's house. The very same logic may be applied to the cake and the stone examples.

As we see, it is not possible for man to transcend his senses and break free of them. In this respect, a man's soul can be exposed to all kinds of representations of physical events although it has no physical body and no material existence and lacks material weight. It is not possible for a person to realise this because he assumes these three-dimensional images to be real and is certain of their existence because, like everybody, he depends on perceptions experienced by his sensory organs.

The famous British philosopher David Hume expresses his thoughts on this fact:

> For my part, when I enter most intimately into what I call myself, I always stumble on some particular perception or other, of heat or cold, light or shade, love or hatred, pain or pleasure. I never can catch myself at any time without a perception, and **never can observe any thing but the perception.**[26]

The Formation of Perceptions in the Brain is Not Philosophy But Scientific Fact

Materialists claim that what we have been saying here is a philosophical view. However, to hold that the "external world", as we call it, is a collection of perceptions is not a matter of philosophy but a plain scientific fact. How the image and feelings form in the brain is taught in medical schools in detail. These facts, proven by 20th-century science particularly physics, clearly show that matter does not have an absolute reality and that, in a sense, everyone is watching the "monitor in his brain".

Everyone who believes in science, be he an atheist, Buddhist, or someone who holds any other view, has to accept this fact. A materialist might deny the existence of a Creator yet he cannot deny this scientific reality.

The inability of Karl Marx, Friedrich Engels, Georges Politzer and others to comprehend such a simple and evident fact is still startling, although the level of scientific understanding of their times was perhaps insufficient. In our time, science and technology are highly advanced and recent discoveries make it easier to comprehend this fact. Materialists, on the other hand, are flooded with the fear of both comprehending this fact, even partially, and realising how definitely it demolishes their philosophy.

The Great Fear of the Materialists

For a while, no substantial response came from materialist Turkish circles on the subject brought up in this book, that is, the fact that matter is a mere perception. This gave us the impression that our point had not been made so clear and that it needed further explanation. Yet, before long, it was revealed that materialists felt quite uneasy about the popularity of this subject and felt a great fear of it.

For some time, materialists have been loudly proclaiming their fear and panic in their publications, conferences and panels. Their agitated and hopeless discourses imply that they are suffering a severe intellectual crisis. The scientific collapse of the theory of evolution, the so-called basis of their philosophy, had already come as a great shock to them. Now, they come to realise that they start to lose matter itself, which is a greater mainstay for them than Darwinism, and they are experiencing an even greater shock. They declare that this issue is the "biggest threat" to them and that it totally "demolishes their cultural fabric".

One of those who expressed most outspokenly the anxiety and panic felt by materialist circles was Renan Pekunlu, an academician as well as writer of the *Bilim ve Utopya* (Science and Utopia) periodical which has assumed the task of defending materialism. Both in his articles in Bilim ve Utopya and in the panels he attended, Pekunlu presented the book *Evolution Deceit* by Harun Yahya as the number one "threat" to materialism. What disturbed Pekunlu even more than the chapters that invalidated Darwinism was the part you are currently reading. To his readers and audience, the latter of whom were only a handful, Pekunlu delivered the message "do not let yourselves be carried away by the indoctrination of idealism and keep your faith in materialism". He quoted Vladimir I. Lenin, the leader of the bloody communist revolution in Russia, as reference. Advising everyone to read Lenin's century-old book titled *Materialism and Empirio-Criticism*, Pekunlu repeated the counsels of Lenin, "do not think over this issue, or you will lose track of materialism and be carried away by religion". In an article he wrote in the aforementioned periodical, he quoted the following lines from Lenin:

> Once you deny objective reality, given us in sensation, you have already lost every weapon against fideism, for you have slipped into agnosticism or subjectivism – and that is all that fideism requires. **A single claw ensnared, and the bird is lost.** And our Machists have all become ensnared in idealism, that is, in a diluted, subtle fideism; they became ensnared from the moment they

took "sensation" not as an image of the external world but as a special "element". It is nobody's sensation, nobody's mind, nobody's spirit, nobody's will.[27]

These words clearly demonstrate that the fact which Lenin, in alarm, realised and wanted to take out both of his mind and the minds of his "comrades", also disturbs contemporary materialists in a similar way. However, Pekunlu and other materialists suffer a yet greater distress; because they are aware that this fact is now being put forward in a far more explicit, certain and convincing way than 100 years ago. It is for the first time in world history that this subject is being explained in such an irresistible way.

Nevertheless, the general picture is that a great number of materialist scientists still take a very superficial stand against the fact that "matter is nothing but an illusion". The subject explained in this chapter is **one of the most important and most exciting subjects** that one can ever come across in his life. There is no chance of them having faced such a crucial subject before. Still, the reactions of these scientists or the manner they employ in their speeches and articles hint at how shallow and superficial their comprehension is.

The reactions of some materialists to the subject discussed here show that their blind adherence to materialism has caused some kind of harm to their logic. For this reason, they are far removed from comprehending the subject. For instance, Alaattin Senel, also an academician and writer for *Bilim ve Utopya*, expressed similar sentiments as Rennan Pekunlu saying, **"Forget the collapse of Darwinism, the really threatening subject is this one"**. Sensing that his own philosophy has no basis, he made demands such as "prove what you say!" More interestingly, this writer has himself written lines revealing that he cannot grasp this fact, which he considers a menace.

Turkish materialist writer Rennan Pekunlu says that "the theory of evolution is not so important, the real threat is this subject", because he is aware that this subject nullifies matter, the only concept in which he has faith.

For instance, in an article in which he discussed this subject exclusively, Senel accepts that the external world is perceived in the brain as an image. However, he then goes on to claim that images are divided into two: those having physical correlates and those that do not, and that images pertaining to the external world have physical correlates. In order to support his assertion, he gives "the example of the telephone". In summary, he wrote: "I do not know whether the images in my brain have correlates in the external world or not, but the same thing applies when I speak on the phone. When I speak on the telephone, I cannot see the person I am speaking to but I can have this conversation confirmed when I later see him face to face."[28]

By saying so, this writer actually means the following: "If we doubt our perceptions, we can look at the matter itself and check its reality." However, this is an evident misconception because it is impossible for us to reach the matter itself. **We can never get out of our mind and know what is "outside".** Whether the voice on the telephone has a correlate or not can be confirmed by the person on the other end. However, this confirmation is also imagery, which is experienced in the mind.

These people also experience the same events in their dreams. For instance, Senel may also see in his dream that he speaks on the telephone and then have this conversation confirmed by the person to whom he spoke. Pekunlu may in his dream feel himself facing "a serious threat" and advising people to read century-old books of Lenin. However, no matter what they do, these materialists can never deny that the events they have experienced and the people they have talked to in their dreams are nothing but perceptions.

Who, then, will confirm whether the images in the brain have correlates or not? The shadow beings in the brain? Without doubt, it is impossible for materialists to find a source of information that can yield data concerning the outside of the brain and confirm it.

Conceding that all perceptions are formed in the brain but assuming that one can step "out" of this and have the perceptions confirmed by the real external world reveals that the intellectual capacity of the person is limited and that his reasoning is distorted.

However, any person with a normal level of understanding and reasoning can easily grasp these facts. Every unbiased person knows, in relation to all that we have said, that it is not possible for him to test the existence of the external world with his senses. Yet, it appears that blind adherence to materialism distorts the reasoning capacity of people. For this reason, contemporary materialists display severe logical flaws in their reasoning just like their mentors who tried to "prove" the existence of matter by kicking stones or eating cakes.

It also has to be said that this is not an astonishing situation, because inability to understand is a common trait of all unbelievers. In the Qur'an, Allah particularly states that they are **"a people without understanding"** (Surat al-Ma'idah: 58)

Materialists Have Fallen into the Biggest Trap in History

The atmosphere of panic sweeping through materialist circles in Turkey, of which we have here mentioned only a few examples, shows that materialists face utter defeat, which they have never met before in history. That matter is simply a perception has been proven by modern science and it is put forward in a very clear, straightforward and forceful way. It only remains for materialists to see and acknowledge the collapse of the entire material world in which they blindly believe and on which they rely.

Materialist thought has always existed throughout the history of humanity. Being very assured of themselves and the philosophy they believe in, they revolted against Allah who created them. The scenario they formulated maintained that matter has no beginning or end, and that all these could not possibly have a Creator. Because of their arrogance, they denied Allah and took refuge in matter, which they held to have real existence. They were so confident in this philosophy that they thought that it would never be possible to put forth an explanation proving the contrary.

That is why the facts told in this book regarding the real nature of matter surprised these people so much. What has been told here destroyed the very basis of their philosophy and left no ground for further discussion. Matter, upon which they based all their thoughts, lives, their arrogance and denial, vanished all of a sudden. **How can materialism exist when matter does not?**

One of the attributes of Allah is His plotting against the unbelievers. This is stated in the verse "They plot and plan, and Allah too plans; but **Allah is the best of planners.**" (Surat al- Anfal: 30)

Allah entrapped materialists by making them assume that matter exists and, so doing, humiliated them in an unseen way. Materialists deemed their possessions, status, rank, the society to which they belong, the whole world and everything else to really exist and grew arrogant against Allah by relying on these. They revolted against Allah by being boastful and added to their unbelief. While so doing, they totally relied on matter. Yet, they are so lacking in understanding that they fail to think that Allah encompasses them round about. Allah announces the state to which the unbelievers are led as a result of their thick-headedness:

> Or do they intend a plot (against you)? But **those who defy Allah are themselves involved in a plot!** (Surat at-Tur: 42)

This is most probably their biggest defeat in history. While growing arrogant, materialists have been tricked and suffered a serious defeat in the war they waged against Allah by bringing up something monstrous against Him. The verse "Thus have We placed leaders in every town, its wicked men, to plot therein: but **they only plot against their own souls, and they perceive it not**" announces how unconscious these people who revolt against their Creator are, and how they will end up (Surat al- An'am: 123). In another verse the same fact is related as:

> Fain would they deceive Allah and those who believe, but **they only deceive themselves, and realise (it) not!** (Surat al-Baqarah: 9)

While the unbelievers try to plot, they do not realise a very important fact which is stressed by the words "they only deceive themselves, and realise (it) not!" in the verse. This is the fact that everything they experience is an imagination designed to be perceived by them, and all plots they devise are simply images formed in their brain just like every other act they perform. Their folly has made them forget that they are all alone with Allah and, hence, they are entrapped in their own devious plans.

No less than those unbelievers who lived in the past, those living today face a reality that will shatter their devious plans at their foundations. With the verse **"...feeble indeed is the cunning of Satan"** (Surat an-Nisa: 76), Allah says that these plots were doomed to end with failure the day they were hatched. He gives good tidings to believers with the verse **"...not the least harm will their cunning do you."** (Surat Ali 'Imran: 120)

In another verse Allah says: "But **the unbelievers, their deeds are like a mirage in sandy deserts,** which the man parched with thirst mistakes for water; until when he comes up to it, he finds it to be nothing." (Surat an-Nur: 39). Materialism, too, becomes a "mirage" for the rebellious just as it is stated in this verse; when they have recourse to it, they find it to be nothing but an illusion. Allah has deceived them with such a mirage, and beguiled them into perceiving this whole collection of images as real. All those "eminent" people, professors, astronomers, biologists, physicists, and all others regardless of their rank and post are simply deceived like children, and are humiliated because they took matter as their god. Assuming a collection of images to be absolute, they based their philosophy and ideology on it, became involved in serious discussions, and adopted so-called "intellectual" discourse. They deemed themselves wise enough to offer an argument about the truth of the universe and, more importantly, to dispute about Allah with their limited intelligence. Allah explains their situation in the following verse:

> And (the unbelievers) plotted and planned, and Allah too planned, and the best of planners is Allah. (Surat Ali 'Imran: 54)

It may be possible to escape from some plots; however, this plan of Allah against the unbelievers is so firm that there is no way of escape from it. No matter what they do or to whom they appeal, they can never find a helper other than Allah. As Allah informs in the Qur'an, **"they shall not find for them other than Allah a patron or a helper."** (Surat an-Nisa: 173)

Materialists never expected to fall into such a trap. Having all the means of the 20th century at their disposal, they thought they could grow obstinate in their denial and drag people to disbelief. Allah describes this everlasting mentality of unbelievers and their end as follows in the Qur'an:

> **They plotted and planned**, but **We too planned, even while they perceived it not.** Then see what was the end of their plot! This, that **We destroyed them and their people, all (of them)**. (Surat an-Naml: 50-51)

And behold! You come to us bare and alone as We created you for the first time: you have left behind you all (the favours) which We bestowed on you... *(Surat al-An'am: 94)*

This, on another level, is what the verses come to mean: materialists are made to realise that everything they own is but an illusion, and therefore **everything they possess has been destroyed**. As they witness their possessions, factories, gold, dollars, children, spouses, friends, rank and status, and even their own bodies, all of which they deem to exist, slipping away from their hands, they are **"destroyed"** in the words of the 51st verse of Surat an-Naml. At this point, they are no more material entities but souls.

No doubt, realising this truth is the worst possible situation for materialists. The fact that everything they possess is only an illusion is tantamount, in their own words, to "death before dying" in this world.

This fact leaves them alone with Allah. With the verse, **"Leave Me alone, (to deal) with the (creature) whom I created (bare and) alone"**, Allah calls us to attend to the fact that each human being is, in truth, all alone in His presence. (Surat al- Muddaththir: 11). This remarkable fact is repeated in many other verses:

> And behold! You come to us **bare and alone** as We created you for the first time: you have left behind you all (the favours) which We bestowed on you... (Surat al-An'am: 94)
>
> And each one of them will come to Him on the Day of Resurrection, **alone**. (Surah Maryam: 95)

This, on another level, is what the verses indicate: those who take matter as their god have come from Allah and returned to Him. They have submitted their wills to Allah whether they want or not. Now they wait for the Day of Judgement when everyone of them will be called to account, however unwilling they may be to understand it.

Conclusion

The subject we have explained so far is one of the greatest truths that you will ever be told in your lifetime. Proving that the whole material world is in reality a **"shadow being"**, this subject is the key to comprehending the being of Allah and His creation and of understanding that He is the only absolute being.

The person who understands this subject realises that the world is not the sort of place it is thought by most people to be. The world is not an absolute place with a true existence as supposed by those who wander aimlessly about the streets, get into fights in pubs, show off in luxurious cafes, brag about their property, or who dedicate their lives to hollow aims. The world is only a collection of perceptions, an illusion. All of the people we have cited above are only shadow beings who watch these perceptions in their minds; yet, they are not aware of this.

This concept is very important for it undermines the **materialist philosophy** that denies the existence of Allah and causes it to collapse. This is the reason why materialists like **Marx**, **Engels**, and **Lenin** felt panic, became enraged, and warned their followers "not to think about" this concept when they were told about it. These people are so mentally deficient that they cannot even comprehend that perceptions are formed inside the brain. They assume that the world they watch in their brain is the "external world" and cannot comprehend obvious evidence to the contrary.

This unawareness is the outcome of the little wisdom Allah has given the disbelievers. As Allah says in the Qur'an, the unbelievers "**have hearts wherewith they understand not,** eyes wherewith they see not, and ears wherewith they hear not. They are like cattle – nay more misguided, for they are heedless (of warning)." (Surat al-A'raf: 179)

You can explore beyond this point by using the power of your personal reflection. For this, you have to concentrate, devote your attention, and ponder on the way you see the objects around you and the way you feel their touch. If you think heedfully, you can feel that the intelligent being that sees, hears, touches, thinks, and reads this book at this moment is only a soul and watches the perceptions called "matter" on a screen. The person who comprehends this is considered to have moved away from the domain of the material world that deceives a major part of humanity and to have entered the domain of true existence.

This reality has been understood by a number of theists or philosophers throughout history. Islamic intellectuals such as Imam Rabbani, Muhyiddin Ibn al-'Arabi and Mawlana Jami realised this from the signs of the Qur'an and by using their reason. Some Western philosophers like George Berkeley have grasped the same reality through reason. Imam Rabbani wrote in his Maktubat (Letters) that the whole material universe is an "illusion and supposition (perception)" and that the only absolute being is Allah:

> Allah... The substance of these beings which He created is but nothingness... He created all in **the sphere of senses and illusions...** The existence of the universe is in the sphere of senses and illusions, and it is not material... In reality, there is nothing in the outside except the Glorious Being, (Who is Allah).[29]

Imam Rabbani explicitly stated that all images presented to man are only illusions, and that they have no originals in the "outside".

> This imaginary cycle is portrayed in imagination. It is seen to the extent that it is portrayed, yet, **with the mind's eye**. In the outside, it seems as if it is seen with the head's eye. However, the case is not so. It has neither a designation nor a trace in the outside. There is no circumstance to be seen. Even the face of a person reflected in a mirror is like that. It has no constancy in the outside. No doubt, both its constancy and image are in the **IMAGINATION.** Allah knows best.[30]

Mawlana Jami stated the same fact, which he discovered by following the signs of the Qur'an and by using his wit: **"Whatever there is in the universe are senses and illusions.** They are either like reflections in mirrors or shadows".

However, the number of those who have understood this fact throughout history has always been limited. Great scholars such as Imam Rabbani have written that it might not be wise to tell this fact to the masses because most people are not able to grasp it.

In the age in which we live, this has been made an empirical fact by the body of evidence put forward by science. The fact that the universe is a shadow being is described in such a concrete, clear, and explicit way for the first time in history.

For this reason, the **21st century will be a historical turning-point** when people will generally comprehend the divine realities and be led in crowds to Allah, the only Absolute Being. The materialistic creeds of the 19th century will be relegated to the trash-heaps of history, Allah's being and creating will be grasped, spacelessness and timelessness will be understood, humanity will break free of the centuries-old veils, deceits and superstitions confusing them.

It is not possible for this unavoidable course to be impeded by any shadow being.

Relativity of Time and the Reality of Fate

Everything related above demonstrates that "three-dimensional space" does not exist in reality, that it is a prejudice completely founded on perceptions and that one leads one's whole life in "spacelessness". To assert the contrary would be to hold a superstitious belief far removed from reason and scientific truth, for there is no valid proof of the existence of a three-dimensional material world.

This refutes the primary assumption of the materialist philosophy that underlies evolutionary theory, the assumption that matter is absolute and eternal. The second assumption upon which materialistic philosophy rests is the supposition that time is absolute and eternal. This is as superstitious as the first.

The Perception of Time

What we perceive as time is, in fact, a method by which one moment is compared to another. We can explain this with an example. For instance, when a person taps an object, he hears a particular sound. When he taps the same object five minutes later, he hears another sound. The person perceives that there is an interval between the first sound and the second and he calls this interval "time". Yet at the time he hears the second sound, the first sound he heard is no more than an imagination in his mind. It is merely a bit of information in his memory. The person formulates the concept of "time" by **comparing the moment in which he lives with what** he has in his memory. **If this comparison is not made, there can be no concept of time.**

Similarly, a person makes a comparison when he sees someone entering a room through a door and sitting in an armchair in the middle of the room. By the time this person sits in the armchair, the images related to the moments he opens the door, walks into the room, and makes his way to the armchair are compiled as bits of information in the brain. The perception of time occurs when one compares the man sitting in the armchair with those bits of information.

In brief, **time comes to exist as a result of the comparison made between some illusions stored in the brain.** If man did not have memory, then his brain would not make such interpretations and therefore would never have formed the concept of time. The only reason why someone determines himself to be thirty years old is because he has accumulated information pertaining to those thirty years in his mind. If his memory did not exist, then he would not think of the existence of such a preceding period and he would only experience the single "moment" in which he lives.

The Scientific Explanation of Timelessness

Let us try to clarify the subject by quoting various scientists' and scholars' explanations of the subject. Regarding the subject of time flowing backwards, the famous intellectual and Nobel laureate professor of genetics, François Jacob, states the following in his book *Le Jeu des Possibles* (The Possible and the Actual):

> Films played backwards make it possible for us to imagine **a world in which time flows backwards**. A world in which milk separates itself from the coffee and jumps out of the cup to reach the milk-pan; a world in which light rays are emitted from the walls to be collected in a trap (gravity center) instead of gushing out from a light source; a world in which a stone slopes to the palm of a man by the astonishing cooperation of innumerable drops of water making the stone possible to jump out of water. Yet, in such a world in which time has such opposite features, **the processes of our brain and the way our memory compiles information, would similarly be func-**

tioning backwards. The same is true for the past and future and the world will appear to us exactly as it currently appears.[31]

Since our brain is accustomed to a certain sequence of events, the world operates not as is related above and we assume that time always flows forward. However, this is a decision reached in the brain and is relative. In reality, we can never know how time flows or even whether it flows or not. This is an indication of the fact that **time is not an absolute fact but just a sort of perception.**

The relativity of time is a fact also verified by one of the most important physicists of the 20th century, Albert Einstein. Lincoln Barnett, writes in his book The Universe and Dr. Einstein:

> Along with absolute space, Einstein discarded the concept of absolute time – of a steady, unvarying inexorable universal time flow, streaming from the infinite past to the infinite future. Much of the obscurity that has surrounded the Theory of Relativity stems from man's reluctance to recognize that sense of **time, like sense of color, is a form of perception**. Just as space is simply a possible order of material objects, so **time is simply a possible order of events**. The subjectivity of time is best explained in Einstein's own words. "The experiences of an individual" he says, "appear to us arranged in a series of events; in this series **the single events which we remember appear to be ordered according to the criterion of 'earlier' and 'later'.** There exists, therefore, for the individual, an I-time, or **subjective time**. This in itself is not measurable. I can, indeed, associate numbers with the events, in such a way that a greater number is associated with the later event than with an earlier one.[32]

Einstein himself pointed out, as quoted in Barnett's book: "space and time are forms of intuition, which **can no more be divorced from consciousness** than can our concepts of colour, shape, or size." According to the Theory of General Relativity: **"time has no independent existence apart from the order of events by which we measure it."**[33]

Since time consists of perception, it depends entirely on the perceiver and is therefore relative.

The speed at which time flows differs according to the references we use to measure it because there is no natural clock in the human body to indicate precisely how fast time passes. As Lincoln Barnett wrote: "Just as there is no such thing as color without an eye to discern it, so an instant or an hour or a day is nothing without an event to mark it."[34]

The relativity of time is plainly experienced in dreams. Although what we see in our dreams seems to last for hours, in fact, it only lasts for a few minutes, and even a few seconds.

Let us think about an example to clarify the subject further. Let us assume that we were put in a room with a single window that was specifically designed and we were kept there for a certain period. Let there be a clock in the room from which we can see the amount of time that has passed. At the same time, let it be that we see from the window of the room the sun rising and setting at certain intervals. A few days later, the answer we would give to the question about the amount of time we spent in the room would be based both on the information we had collected by looking at the clock from time to time and on the computation we had made by referring to how many times the sun rose and set. For example, we estimate that we spent three days in the room. However, if the person who put us in that room said that we spent only two days in the room and that the sun we had seen from the window was produced artificially by a simulation machine and that the clock in the room was regulated specially to work faster, then the calculation we had done would have no meaning.

This example confirms that the information we have about the rate of passage of time is based on relative references. The relativity of time is a scientific fact also proven by scientific methodology. **Einstein's Theory of General Relativity** maintains that the speed of time changes depending on the speed of the object and its position in the gravitational field. As speed increases, time is shortened and compressed: it slows down as if coming to the point of "stopping".

Let us explain this with an example given by Einstein. Imagine two twins, one of whom stays on earth while the other goes travelling in space at a speed close to that of light. When he comes back, the traveller will see that his brother has grown much older than he has. The reason is that time flows much slower for the person who travels at speeds near the speed of light. Let us consider a space-travelling father and his earth-bound son. If the father was twenty-seven years old when he set out and his son three; when the father came back to earth thirty years later (earth time), the son would be thirty-three years old while his father would only be thirty.[35] This relativity of time is not caused by the deceleration or acceleration of clocks, or the deceleration of a mechanical spring. It is rather the result of the differentiated operation periods of the entire system of material existence, which goes as deep as sub-atomic particles. In other words, for the person experiencing it, the shortening of time is not experienced as if acting in a slow-motion picture. In such a setting where time shortens, one's heartbeats, cell replications, and brain functions, etc, all operate slower than those of the slower-moving person on Earth. Nevertheless, the person goes on with his daily life and does not notice the shortening of time at all. Indeed the shortening does not even become apparent until comparison is made.

Relativity in the Qur'an

The conclusion to which we are led by the findings of modern science is that **time is not an absolute fact as supposed by materialists, but only a relative perception.** What is most interesting is that this fact, undiscovered until the 20th century by science, was revealed to mankind in the Qur'an fourteen centuries ago. There are various references in the Qur'an to the relativity of time.

It is possible to see in many verses of the Qur'an the scientifically-proven fact that time is a psychological perception dependent on events, the setting, and conditions. For instance, a person's entire life is a very short time as we are informed in the Qur'an:

> On the Day when He will call you, and you will answer (His Call) with (words of) His Praise and Obedience, and you will think that you have stayed (in this world) **but a little while**! (Surat al-Isra: 52)
> And on the Day when He shall gather them together, (it will seem to them) as if they had not tarried (on earth) **longer than an hour of a day**: they will recognise each other. (Surah Yunus: 45)

Some verses indicate that people perceive time differently and that sometimes people can perceive a very short period as a very lengthy one. The following conversation of people held during their judgement in the Hereafter is a good example of this:

He will say: "What number of years did you stay on earth?" They will say: "We stayed **a day or part of a day**, but ask those who keep account." He will say: "You stayed not but a little, if you had only known!" (Surat al-Muminun: 112-114)

In some other verses Allah states that time may flow at different paces in different settings:

Yet, they ask you to hasten on the Punishment! But Allah will not fail in His Promise. Verily **a Day in the sight of your Lord is like a thousand years of your reckoning.** (Surat al-Hajj: 47)

The angels and the spirit ascend unto Him in **a day the measure whereof is (as) fifty thousand years.** (Surat al-Ma'arij: 4)

He rules (all) affairs from the heavens to the earth: in the end will (all affairs) ascend to Him in **a day the measure of which is a thousand years of what you count.** (Surat al-Sajda, 5)

These verses are clear expressions of the relativity of time. That this result, which was only recently understood by scientists in the 20th century, was communicated to man 1,400 years ago in the Qur'an is an indication of the revelation of the Qur'an by Allah, Who encompasses the whole of time and space.

Many other verses of the Qur'an reveal that time is a perception. This is particularly evident in the stories. For instance, Allah has kept the Companions of the Cave, a group of believing people mentioned in the Qur'an, in a deep sleep for more than three centuries. When they awoke, these people thought that they had stayed in that state but a little while, and could not reckon how long they had slept:

Then We drew (a veil) over their ears, for a number of years, in the Cave, (so that they heard not). Then We raised them up that We might know which of the two parties would best calculate the time that they had tarried. (Surat al-Kahf: 11-12)

Such (being their state), We raised them up (from sleep), that they might question each other. Said one of them, "How long have you stayed (here)?" They said, "We have stayed (perhaps) a day, or part of a day." (At length)

they (all) said, "Allah (alone) knows best how long you have stayed here..."
(Surat al-Kahf: 19)

The situation told in the below verse below is also evidence that time is in truth a psychological perception.

> Or (take) the similitude of one who passed by a hamlet, all in ruins to its roofs. He said, "How shall Allah bring it (ever) to life, after (this) its death?" but Allah caused him to die for a hundred years, then raised him up (again). He said: "How long did you tarry (thus)?" He said: (Perhaps) a day or part of a day." He said: "Nay, you have tarried thus a hundred years; but look at your food and your drink; they show no signs of age; and look at your donkey. And that We may make of you a sign unto the people, Look further at the bones, how We bring them together and clothe them with flesh." When this was shown clearly to him, he said: "I know that Allah has power over all things." (Surat al-Baqara: 259)

The above verse clearly emphasises that Allah Who created time is unbound by it. Man, on the other hand, is bound by time, which is ordained by Allah. As in the verse, man is even incapable of knowing how long he slept. In such a state, to assert that time is absolute (just as materialists, in their distorted thinking, do) is very unreasonable.

Destiny

This relativity of time clears up a very important matter. Relativity is so variable that a period appearing billions of years' duration to us may last only a second in another perspective. Moreover, an enormous period of time extending from the world's beginning to its end may not even last a second but just an instant in another dimension.

This is the very essence of the concept of destiny – a concept that is not well understood by most people, especially materialists who deny it completely. Destiny is Allah's perfect knowledge of all events past or future. A majority of people question how Allah can already know events that have not yet been experienced and this leads them to fail in understanding the authenticity of destiny. However, "events not yet experienced" are only so **for us**. Allah is not bound by time or space for He Himself has created them. For this reason, **past, future, and present are all the same**

to Allah; for Him everything has already taken place and finished.

In *The Universe and Dr. Einstein*, Lincoln Barnett explains how the Theory of General Relativity leads to this conclusion. According to Barnett, the universe can be **"encompassed in its entire majesty only by a cosmic intellect"**.[36] The will that Barnett calls "the cosmic intellect" is **the wisdom and knowledge of Allah, Who prevails over the entire universe.** Just as we can easily see a ruler's beginning, middle, and end, and all the units in between as a whole, Allah knows the time we are subject to as if it were a single moment right from its beginning to its end. People, however, experience incidents only when their time comes and they witness the destiny Allah has created for them.

It is also important to draw attention to the shallowness of the distorted understanding of destiny prevalent in our society. This distorted belief of fate is a superstition that Allah has determined a "destiny" for every man but that these destinies can sometimes be changed by people. For instance, people make superficial statements about a patient who returns from death's door such as "he defeated his destiny". No-one is able to change his destiny. The person who returned from death's door, didn't die precisely because he was destined not to die at that time. It is, ironically, the destiny of those people who deceive themselves by saying "I defeated my destiny" that they should say so and maintain such a mindset.

Destiny is the eternal knowledge of Allah and for Allah, Who knows time like a single moment and Who prevails over the whole of time and space; everything is determined and finished in destiny. We also understand from what He relates in the Qur'an that time is one for Allah: some incidents that appear to us to happen in the future are related in the Qur'an in such a way as if they had already taken place long before. For instance, the verses that describe the accounts that people must give to Allah in the hereafter are related as events which occurred long ago:

> And the trumpet **is blown**, and all who are in the heavens and all who are in the earth **swoon away**, save him whom Allah wills. Then it **is blown** a second time, and behold them standing waiting! And the earth **shone** with the light of her Lord, and the Book is set up, and the prophets and the witnesses **are brought**, and it **is judged** between them with truth, and they **are**

not wronged... And those who disbelieve **are driven** unto hell in troops...: And those who feared their Lord **are driven** unto Paradise in troops" (Surat az-Zumar: 68-73)

Some other verses on this subject are:

And every soul **came**, along with it a driver and a witness. (Surat al-Qaf: 21)

And the heaven **is cloven asunder**, so that on that day it **is frail**. (Surat al-Haqqah: 16)

And because they were patient and constant, He rewarded them with a Garden and (garments of) silk. Reclining in the (Garden) on raised thrones, they **saw** there neither the sun's (excessive heat) nor excessive cold. (Surat al-Insan: 12-13)

And Hell **is placed** in full view for (all) to see. (Surat an-Nazi'at: 36)

But on this Day the believers **laugh** at the unbelievers (Surat al-Mutaffifin: 34)

And the Sinful **saw** the Fire and **apprehended** that they have to fall therein: no means **did they find** to turn away therefrom. (Surat al-Kahf: 53)

As may be seen, occurrences that are going to take place after our death (from our point of view) are related in the Qur'an as past events already experienced. Allah is not bound by the relative time frame in which we are confined. Allah has willed these things in timelessness: people have already performed them and all these events have been lived through and are ended. He imparts in the verse below that every event, big or small, is within the knowledge of Allah and recorded in a book:

In whatever business you may be, and whatever portion you may be reciting from the Qur'an, and whatever deed you (mankind) may be doing, We are witnesses thereof when you are deeply engrossed therein. Nor is hidden from your Lord (so much as) the weight of an atom on the earth or in heaven. And not the least and not the greatest of these things but are recorded in a clear record. (Surah Yunus: 61)

The Worry of the Materialists

The issues discussed in this chapter, namely the truth underlying matter, timelessness, and spacelessness, are indeed extremely clear. As expressed before, these are definitely not any sort of philosophy or way of thought, but **scientific outcomes that are impossible to deny**. In addition to its being a technical reality, the evidence also admits of no other rational and logical alternatives on this issue: **the universe** is an **illusory entity** with all the matter composing it and all the creatures living in it. It is a collection of perceptions.

Materialists have a hard time understanding this issue. For instance, if we return to Politzer's bus example: although Politzer technically knew that he could not step out of his perceptions he could only admit it in certain cases. That is, for Politzer, events take place in the brain until the bus crash, but as soon as the bus crash takes place, things go out of the brain and gain a physical reality. The logical defect of this point is very clear. Politzer has made the same mistake as the materialist Johnson who said, "I hit the stone, my foot hurts, therefore it exists". Politzer could not understand that the shock felt after the impact of the bus was merely a perception as well.

The subliminal reason why materialists cannot comprehend this subject is their fear of what they will face when they comprehend it. Lincoln Barnett tells us that some scientists "discerned" this subject:

> Along with philosophers' reduction of all objective reality to a shadow-world of perceptions, scientists have become aware of the **alarming** limitations of man's senses.[37]

Any reference made to the fact that matter and time are perceptions arouses great fear in the materialist, because these are the only notions he relies on as absolute beings. He, in a sense, takes them as idols to worship; because he thinks that matter and time (through evolution) created him.

When he feels that the universe in which he thinks he is living, the world, his own body, other people, other materialist philosophers by whose ideas he is influenced, and, in short, everything is a perception, he feels overwhelmed by a horror at it all. Everything he depends on, believes in, and has recourse to suddenly vanishes. He feels a taste of the desperation which he will really experience on the Day of Judgement, as described in the verse "That Day shall they (openly) show (their) submission to Allah; and **all their inventions left them in the lurch.**" (Surat an-Nahl: 87)

From then on, this materialist tries to convince himself of the reality of matter, and makes up "evidence" for this end. He hits his fist on the wall, kicks stones, shouts, yells, but can never escape from the reality.

Just as they want to dismiss this reality from their minds, they also want other people to discard it. They are also aware that if people in general know the true nature of matter, the primitive nature of their own philosophy and the ignorance of their worldview will be bared for all to see, and there will be no ground left on which they can found their views. These fears are the reasons why they are so disturbed at the facts related here.

Allah states that the fears of the unbelievers will be intensified in the hereafter. On the Day of Judgement, they will be addressed thus:

> One day shall We gather them all together. We shall say to those who ascribed partners (to Us): **"Where are the partners whom you (invented and) talked about?"** (Surat al-An'am: 22)

After that, unbelievers will witness their possessions, children and their intimates, whom they had assumed to be real and had ascribed as partners to Allah, leaving them and vanishing. Allah informs us of this in the verse **"Behold! How they lie against their own selves! But the (lie) which they invented left them in the lurch."** (Surat al-An'am: 24).

The Gain of Believers

While the fact that matter and time are perceptions alarms materialists, the opposite holds true for believers. People of faith become very glad when they perceive the secret behind matter, because this reality is the key to all questions. With this key, all secrets are unlocked. One comes easily to understand many issues that one previously had difficulty in understanding.

As said before, the questions of death, paradise, hell, the hereafter, changing dimensions, and questions such as "Where is Allah?" "What was before Allah?" "Who created Allah?" "How long will life in the grave last?" "Where are heaven and hell?" and "Where do heaven and hell currently exist?" are easily answered. It will be understood with what kind of order Allah created the entire universe from out of nothing, so much so that, with this secret, **the questions of "when?" and "where?" become meaning-less** because there are no time and no space left. When spacelessness is grasped, it will be understood that hell, heaven and earth are all actually **the same place**. If timelessness is grasped, it will be understood that everything takes place at **a single moment**: nothing is waited for and time does not go by, because everything has already happened and finished.

With this secret delved, **the world becomes like heaven for a believer.** All distressful material worries, anxieties, and fears vanish. The person grasps that the entire universe has a single Sovereign, that He changes the entire physical world as He pleases and that all one has to do is to turn to Him. He then submits himself entirely to Allah **"to be devoted to His service"**. (Surat Ali 'Imran: 35)

To comprehend this secret is the greatest gain in the world.

With this secret, another very important reality mentioned in the Qur'an is unveiled: that **"Allah is nearer to man than his jugular vein"** (Surah Qaf: 16). As everybody knows, the jugular vein is inside the body. What could be nearer to a person than his inside? This situation can easily be explained by the reality of spacelessness. This verse also can be much better comprehended by understanding this secret.

This is the plain truth. It should be well established that there is no helper and provider for man other than Allah. **There is nothing but Allah;** He is the only absolute being with Whom one can seek refuge, to Whom one can appeal for help and count on for reward.

Wherever we turn, there is the presence of Allah.

The Evolution Deceit

The theory of evolution is a philosophy and a conception of the world that produces false hypotheses, assumptions and imaginary scenarios in order to explain the existence and origin of life in terms of mere coincidences. The roots of this philosophy go back as far as antiquity and ancient Greece.

All atheist philosophies that deny creation, directly or indirectly embrace and defend the idea of evolution. The same condition today applies to all the ideologies and systems that are antagonistic to religion.

The evolutionary notion has been cloaked in a scientific disguise for the last century and a half in order to justify itself. Though put forward as a supposedly scientific theory during the mid-19th century, the theory, despite all the best efforts of its advocates, has not so far been verified by any scientific finding or experiment. Indeed, the "very science" on which the theory depends so greatly has demonstrated and continues to demonstrate repeatedly that the theory has no merit in reality.

Laboratory experiments and probabilistic calculations have definitely made it clear that the amino acids from which life arises cannot have been formed by chance. The cell, which supposedly emerged by chance under primitive and uncontrolled terrestrial conditions according to evolutionists, still cannot be synthesised even in the most sophisticated, high-tech laboratories of the 20th century. Not a single "transitional form", creatures which are supposed to show the gradual evolution of advanced organisms from more primitive ones as neo-Darwinist theory claims, has ever been found anywhere in the world despite the most diligent and prolonged search in the fossil record.

Striving to gather evidence for evolution, evolutionists have unwittingly proven by their own hands that evolution cannot have happened at all!

The person who originally put forward the theory of evolution, essentially in the form that it is defended today, was an amateur English biologist by the name of Charles Robert Darwin. Darwin first published his ideas in a book entitled *The Origin of Species by Means of Natural Selection* in 1859. Darwin claimed in his book that all living beings had a common ancestor and that they evolved from one another by means of natural selection. Those that best adapted to the habitat transferred their traits to subsequent generations, and by accumulating over great epochs, these advantageous qualities transformed individuals into totally different species from their ancestors. The human being was thus the most developed product of the mechanism of natural selection. In short, the origin of one species was another species.

Darwin's fanciful ideas were seized upon and promoted by certain ideological and political circles and the theory became very popular. The main reason was that the level of knowledge of those days was not yet sufficient to reveal that Darwin's imaginary scenarios were false. When Darwin put forward his assumptions, the disciplines of genetics, microbiology, and biochemistry did not yet exist. If they had, Darwin might easily have recognised that his theory was totally unscientific and thus would not have attempted to advance such meaningless claims: the information determining species already exists in the genes and it is impossible for natural selection to produce new species by altering genes.

Charles Darwin

While the echoes of Darwin's book reverberated, an Austrian botanist by the name of Gregor Mendel discovered the laws of inheritance in 1865. Although little known before the end of the century, Mendel's discovery gained great importance in the early 1900s with the birth of the science of genetics. Some time later, the structures of genes and chromosomes were discovered. The discovery, in the 1950s, of the DNA molecule, which incorporates genetic information, threw the theory of evolution into a great crisis, because the origin of the immense amount of information in DNA could not possibly be explained by coincidental happenings.

Besides all these scientific developments, no transitional forms, which were supposed to show the gradual evolution of living organisms from primitive to advanced species, have ever been found despite years of search.

These developments ought to have resulted in Darwin's theory being banished to the dustbin of history. However, it was not, because certain circles insisted on revising, renewing, and elevating the theory to a scientific platform. These efforts gain meaning only if we realise that behind the theory lie ideological intentions rather than scientific concerns.

Nevertheless, some circles that believed in the necessity of upholding a theory that had reached an impasse soon set up a new model. The name of this new model was neo-Darwinism. According to this theory, species evolved as a result of mutations, minor changes in their genes, and the fittest ones survived through the mechanism of natural selection. When, however, it was proved that the mechanisms proposed by neo-Darwinism were invalid and minor changes were not sufficient for the formation of living beings, evolutionists went on to look for new models. They came up with a new claim called "punctuated equilibrium" which rests on no rational or scientific grounds. This model held that living beings suddenly evolved into another species without any transitional forms. In other words, species with no evolutionary "ancestors" suddenly appeared. This was a way of describing creation, though evolutionists would be loath to admit this. They tried to cover it up with incomprehensible scenarios. For instance, they said that the first bird in history could all of a sudden inexplicably have popped out of a reptile egg. The same theory also held that carnivorous land-dwelling animals could have turned into giant whales having undergone a sudden and comprehensive transformation.

These claims, totally contradicting all the rules of genetics, biophysics, and biochemistry are as scientific as fairy-tales of frogs turning into princes! Nevertheless, being distressed by the crisis that the neo-Darwinist assertion was in, some evolutionist paleontologists embraced this theory, which has the distinction of being even more bizarre than neo-Darwinism itself.

The only purpose of this model was to provide an explanation for the gaps in the fossil-record that the neo-Darwinist model could not explain. However, it is hardly rational to attempt to explain the gap in the fossil record of the evolution of birds with a claim that "a bird popped all of a sudden out of a reptile egg", because, by the evolutionists' own admission, the evolution of a species to another species requires a great and advantageous change in genetic information. However, no mutation whatsoever improves the genetic information or adds new information to it. Mutations only derange genetic information. Thus, the "gross mutations" imagined by the punctuated equilibrium model, would only cause "gross", that is "great", reductions and impairments in the genetic information.

The theory of punctuated equilibrium was obviously merely a product of the imagination. Despite this evident truth, the advocates of evolution did not hesitate to honour this theory. The fact that the model of evolution proposed by Darwin could not be proved by the fossil record forced them to do so. Darwin claimed that species underwent a gradual change, which necessitated the existence of half bird-half reptile or half fish-half reptile freaks. However, not even one of these "transitional forms" was found despite the extensive studies of evolutionists and the hundreds of thousands of fossils that were unearthed.

Evolutionists seized upon the model of punctuated equilibrium with the hope of concealing this great fossil fiasco. As we have stated before, it was very evident that this theory is a fantasy, so it very soon consumed itself. The model of punctuated equilibrium was never put forward as a consistent model, but rather used as an escape in cases that plainly did not fit the model of gradual evolution. Since evolutionists today realise that complex organs such as eyes, wings, lungs, brain and others explicitly refute the model of gradual evolution, in these particular points they are compelled to take shelter in the fantastic interpretations of the model of punctuated equilibrium.

Is there any Fossil Record to Verify the Theory of Evolution?

The theory of evolution argues that the evolution of a species into another species takes place gradually, step-by-step over millions of years. The logical inference drawn from such a claim is that monstrous living organisms called "transitional forms" should have lived during these periods of transformation. Since evolutionists allege that all living things evolved from each other step-by-step, the number and variety of these transitional forms should have been in the millions.

If such creatures had really lived, then we should see their remains everywhere. In fact, if this thesis is correct, the number of intermediate transitional forms should be even greater than the number of animal species alive today and their fossilised remains should be abundant all over the world.

Since Darwin, evolutionists have been searching for fossils and the result has been for them a crushing disappointment. Nowhere in the world – neither on land nor in the depths of the sea – has any intermediate transitional form between any two species ever been uncovered.

Darwin himself was quite aware of the absence of such transitional forms. It was his greatest hope that they would be found in the future. Despite his hopefulness, he saw that the biggest stumbling block to his theory was the missing transitional forms. This is why, in his book *The Origin of Species*, he wrote:

> Why, if species have descended from other species by fine gradations, do we not everywhere see innumerable transitional forms? Why is not all nature in confusion, instead of the species being, as we see them, well defined?... But, as by this theory innumerable transitional forms must have existed, why do we not find them embedded in countless numbers in the crust of the earth?...

But in the intermediate region, having intermediate conditions of life, why do we not now find closely-linking intermediate varieties? This difficulty for a long time quite confounded me.[38]

Darwin was right to be worried. The problem bothered other evolutionists as well. A famous British paleontologist, Derek V. Ager, admits this embarrassing fact:

The point emerges that if we examine the fossil record in detail, whether at the level of orders or of species, we find – over and over again – not gradual evolution, but the sudden explosion of one group at the expense of another.[39]

The gaps in the fossil record cannot be explained away by the wishful thinking that not enough fossils have yet been unearthed and that these missing fossils will one day be found. Another evolutionist paleontologist, T. Neville George, explains the reason:

There is no need to apologise any longer for the poverty of the fossil record. In some ways, it has become almost unmanageably rich and discovery is outpacing integration... The fossil record nevertheless continues to be composed mainly of gaps.[40]

Life Emerged on Earth Suddenly and in Complex Forms

When terrestrial strata and the fossil record are examined, it is seen that living organisms appeared simultaneously. The oldest stratum of the earth in which fossils of living creatures have been found is that of the "Cambrian", which has an estimated age of 530-520 million years.

Living creatures that are found in the strata belonging to the Cambrian period emerged in the fossil record all of a sudden without any pre-existing ancestors. The vast mosaic of living organisms, made up of such great numbers of complex creatures, emerged so suddenly that this miraculous event is referred to as the "Cambrian Explosion" in scientific literature.

Most of the organisms found in this stratum have highly advanced organs like eyes, or systems seen in organisms with a highly advanced organisation such as gills, circulatory systems, and so on. There is no sign in the fossil record to indicate that these organisms had any ancestors.

A 320-million-year-old cockroach fossil (left). A 360-million-year-old Trilobite fossil (below).

Richard Monestarsky, the editor of *Earth Sciences* magazine, states about the sudden emergence of living species:

> A half-billion years ago the remarkably complex forms of animals that we see today suddenly appeared. This moment, right at the start of Earth's Cambrian Period, some 550 million years ago, marks the evolutionary explosion that filled the seas with the world's first complex creatures. The large animal phyla of today were present already in the early Cambrian and they were as distinct from each other then as they are today.[41]

Not being able to find answers to the question of how earth came to overflow with thousands of different animal species, evolutionists posit an imaginary period of 20 million years before the Cambrian Period to explain how life originated and "the unknown happened". This period is called the "evolutionary gap". No evidence for it has ever been found and the concept is still conveniently nebulous and undefined even today.

In 1984, numerous complex invertebrates were unearthed in

Chengjiang, set in the central Yunnan plateau in the high country of southwest China. Among them were trilobites, now extinct, but no less complex in structure than any modern invertebrate.

The Swedish evolutionist paleontologist, Stefan Bengston, explains the situation as follows:

> If any event in life's history resembles man's creation myths, it is this sudden diversification of marine life when multicellular organisms took over as the dominant actors in ecology and evolution. Baffling (and embarrassing) to Darwin, this event still dazzles us.[42]

The sudden appearance of these complex living beings with no predecessors is no less baffling (and embarrassing) for evolutionists today than it was for Darwin 135 years ago. In nearly a century and a half, they have advanced not one step beyond the point that stymied Darwin.

As may be seen, the fossil record indicates that living things did not evolve from primitive to advanced forms, but instead emerged all of a sudden and in a perfect state. The absence of the transitional forms is not peculiar to the Cambrian period. Not a single transitional form verifying the alleged evolutionary "progression" of vertebrates – from fish to amphibians, reptiles, birds, and mammals – has ever been found. Every living species appears instantaneously and in its current form, perfect and complete, in the fossil record.

In other words, living beings did not come into existence through evolution. They were created.

Evolution Forgeries Deceptions in Drawings

The fossil record is the principle source for those who seek evidence for the theory of evolution. When inspected carefully and without prejudice, the fossil record refutes the theory of evolution rather than supporting it. Nevertheless, misleading interpretations of fossils by evolutionists and their prejudiced representation to the public have given many people the impression that the fossil record indeed supports the theory of evolution.

The susceptibility of some findings in the fossil record to all kinds of interpretations is what best serves the evolutionists' purposes. The fossils unearthed are most of the time unsatisfactory for reliable identification. They usually consist of scattered, incomplete bone fragments. For this reason, it is very easy to distort the available data and to use it as desired. Not surprisingly, the reconstructions (drawings and models) made by evolutionists based on such fossil remains are prepared entirely speculatively in order to confirm evolutionary theses. Since people are readily affected by visual information, these imaginary reconstructed models are employed to convince them that the reconstructed creatures really existed in the past.

Evolutionist researchers draw human-like imaginary creatures, usually setting out from a single tooth, or a mandible fragment or a humerus, and present them to the public in a sensational manner as if they were links in human evolution. These drawings have played a great role in the establishment of the image of "primitive men" in the minds of many people.

These studies based on bone remains can only reveal very general char-

Continuously running into such skilfully drawn half-man half-ape creatures in books or other publications, the public becomes convinced that man evolved from the ape or some similar creature. These drawings, however, are outright forgeries.

acteristics of the creature concerned. The distinctive details are present in the soft tissues that quickly vanish with time. With the soft tissues speculatively interpreted, everything becomes possible within the boundaries of the imagination of the reconstruction's producer. Earnst A. Hooten from Harvard University explains the situation like this:

> To attempt to restore the soft parts is an even more hazardous undertaking. The lips, the eyes, the ears, and the nasal tip leave no clues on the underlying bony parts. You can with equal facility model on a Neanderthaloid skull the features of a chimpanzee or the lineaments of a philosopher. These alleged restorations of ancient types of man have very little if any scientific value and are likely only to mislead the public... So put not your trust in reconstructions.[43]

Studies Made to Fabricate False Fossils

Unable to find valid evidence in the fossil record for the theory of evolution, some evolutionists have ventured to manufacture their own. These efforts, which have even been included in encyclopaedias under the heading "evolution forgeries", are the most telling indication that the theory of evolution is an ideology and a philosophy that evolutionists are hard put to defend. Two of the most egregious and notorious of these forgeries are described below.

Piltdown Man

Charles Dawson, a well-known doctor and amateur paleoanthropologist, came forth with a claim that he had found a jawbone and a cranial fragment in a pit in the area of Piltdown, England in 1912. Although the skull was human-like, the jawbone was distinctly simian. These specimens were christened the "Piltdown Man". Alleged to be 500 thousand years old, they were displayed as absolute proofs of human evolution. For more than 40 years, many scientific articles were written on the "Piltdown Man", many interpretations and drawings were made and the fossil was presented as crucial evidence of human evolution.

In 1949, scientists examined the fossil once more and concluded that the "fossil" was a deliberate forgery consisting of a human skull and the jawbone of an orang-utan.

Using the fluorine dating method, investigators discovered that the skull was only a few thousand years old. The teeth in the jawbone, which belonged to an orang-utan, had been artificially worn down and the "primitive" tools that had conveniently accompanied the fossils were crude forgeries that had been sharpened with steel implements. In the detailed analysis completed by Oakley, Weiner and Clark, they revealed this forgery to the public in 1953. The skull belonged to a 500-year-old man, and the mandibular bone belonged to a recently deceased ape! The teeth were thereafter specially arranged in an array and added to the jaw and the joints were filed in order to make them resemble that of a man. Then all these pieces were stained with potassium dichromate to give them a dated appearance. (These stains disappeared when dipped in acid.) Le Gros Clark, who was a member of the team that disclosed the forgery, could not hide his astonishment:

> The evidences of artificial abrasion immediately sprang to the eye. Indeed so obvious did they seem it may well be asked: how was it that they had escaped notice before? [44]

Nebraska Man

In 1922, Henry Fairfield Osborn, the director of the American Museum of Natural History, declared that he had found a molar tooth fossil in western Nebraska near Snake Brook belonging to the Pliocene period. This tooth allegedly bore the common characteristics of both man and ape.

The above picture was drawn based on a single tooth and it was published in the Illustrated London News of 24th July 1922. However, evolutionists were extremely disappointed when it was revealed that this tooth belonged neither to an ape-like creature nor to a man, but to an extinct species of pig.

Deep scientific arguments began in which some interpreted this tooth to be that of Pithecanthropus erectus while others claimed it was closer to that of modern human beings. This fossil, which aroused extensive debate, was popularly named "Nebraska Man". It was also immediately given a "scientific name": "Hesperopithecus Haroldcooki".

Many authorities gave Osborn their support. Based on this single tooth, reconstructions of Nebraska Man's head and body were drawn. Moreover, Nebraska Man was even pictured with a whole family.

In 1927, other parts of the skeleton were also found. According to these newly discovered pieces, the tooth belonged neither to a man nor to an ape. It was realised that it belonged to an extinct species of wild American pig called Prosthennops.

Did Men and Apes Come from a Common Ancestor?

According to the claims of the theory of evolution, men and modern apes have common ancestors. These creatures evolved in time and some of them became the apes of today while another group that followed another branch of evolution became the men of today.

Evolutionists call the so-called first common ancestors of men and apes "Australopithecus" which means "South African ape". Australopithecus, nothing but an old ape species that has become extinct, has various types. Some of them are robust while others are small and slight.

Evolutionists classify the next stage of human evolution as "Homo", that is "man". According to the evolutionist claim, the living beings in the Homo series are more developed than Australopithecus, and not very much different from modern man. The modern man of our day, Homo sapiens, is said to have formed at the latest stage of the evolution of this species.

The fact of the matter is that the beings called Australopithecus in this imaginary scenario fabricated by evolutionists really are apes that became extinct, and the beings in the Homo series are members of various human races that lived in the past and then disappeared. Evolutionists arranged various ape and human fossils in an order from the smallest to the biggest in order to form a "human evolution" scheme. Research, however, has demonstrated that these fossils by no means imply an evolutionary process and some of these alleged ancestors of man were real apes whereas some of them were real humans.

Now, let us have a look at Australopithecus, which represents to evolutionists the first stage of the scheme of human evolution.

Australopithecus: Extinct Apes

Evolutionists claim that Australopithecus are the most primitive ancestors of modern men. These are an old species with a head and skull structure similar to that of modern apes, yet with a smaller cranial capacity. According to the claims of evolutionists, these creatures have a very important feature that authenticates them as the ancestors of men: bipedalism.

The movements of apes and men are completely different. Human beings are the only living creatures that move freely about on two feet. Some other animals do have a limited ability to move in this way, but those that do have bent skeletons.

According to evolutionists, these living beings called Australopithecus had the ability to walk in a bent rather than an upright posture like human beings. Even this limited bipedal stride was sufficient to encourage evolutionists to project onto these creatures that they were the ancestors of man.

However, the first evidence refuting the allegations of evolutionists that Australopithecus were bipedal came from evolutionists themselves. Detailed studies made on Australopithecus fossils forced even evolutionists to admit that these looked "too" ape-like. Having conducted detailed anatomical research on Australopithecus fossils in the mid-1970s, Charles E. Oxnard likened the skeletal structure of Australopithecus to that of modern orang-utans:

> An important part of today's conventional wisdom about human evolution is based on studies of teeth, jaws and skull fragments of australopithecine fossils. These all indicate that the close relation of the australopithecine to the human lineage may not be true. All these fossils are different from gorillas, chimpanzees and men. Studied as a group, the australopithecine seems more like the orang-utan. [45]

What really embarrassed evolutionists was the discovery that Australopithecus could not have walked on two feet and with a bent posture. It would have been physically very ineffective for Australopithecus, allegedly bipedal but with a bent stride, to move about in such a way because of the enormous energy demands it would have entailed. By means of computer simulations conducted in 1996, the English paleoanthropologist Robin Crompton also demonstrated that such a "compound" stride was impossible. Crompton reached the following conclusion: a living being can walk either upright or on all fours. A type of in-between stride cannot be sustained for long periods because of the extreme energy consumption. This means that Australopithecus could not have been both bipedal and have a bent walking posture.

Probably the most important study demonstrating that Australopithecus could not have been bipedal came in 1994 from the research anatomist Fred Spoor and his team in the Department of Human Anatomy and Cellular Biology at the University of Liverpool, England. This group conducted studies on the bipedalism of fossilised living beings. Their research investigated the involuntary balance mechanism found in the cochlea of the ear, and the findings showed conclusively that Australopithecus could not have been bipedal. This precluded any claims that Australopithecus was human-like.

The Homo Series: Real Human Beings

The next step in the imaginary human evolution is "Homo", that is, the human series. These living beings are humans who are no different from modern men, yet who have some racial differences. Seeking to exaggerate these differences, evolutionists represent these people not as a "race" of modern man but as a different "species". However, as we will soon see, the people in the Homo series are nothing but ordinary human racial types.

According to the fanciful scheme of evolutionists, the internal imaginary evolution of the Homo species is as follows: First Homo erectus, then Homo sapiens archaic and Neanderthal Man, later Cro-Magnon Man and finally modern man.

Despite the claims of evolutionists to the contrary, all the "species" we have enumerated above are nothing but genuine human beings. Let us first examine Homo erectus, who evolutionists refer to as the most primitive human species.

The most striking evidence showing that Homo erectus is not a "primitive" species is the fossil of "Turkana Boy", one of the oldest Homo erectus remains. It is estimated that the fossil was of a 12-year-old boy, who would have been 1.83 meters tall in his adolescence. The upright skeletal structure of the fossil is no different from that of modern man. Its tall and slender skeletal structure totally complies with that of the people living in tropical regions in our day. This fossil is one of the most important pieces of evidence that Homo erectus is simply another specimen of the modern human race. Evolutionist paleontologist Richard Leakey compares Homo erectus and modern man as follows:

> One would also see differences in the shape of the skull, in the degree of protrusion of the face, the robustness of the brows and so on. These differences are probably no more pronounced than we see today between the separate geographical races of modern humans. Such biological variation arises when populations are geographically separated from each other for significant lengths of time.[46]

Leakey means to say that the difference between Homo erectus and us is no more than the difference between Negroes and Eskimos. The cranial features of Homo erectus resulted from their manner of feeding, and genetic emigration and from their not assimilating with other human races for a lengthy period.

Another strong piece of evidence that Homo erectus is not a "primitive" species is that fossils of this species have been unearthed aged twenty-seven thousand years and even thirteen thousand years. According to an article published in Time – which is not a scientific periodical, but nevertheless had a sweeping effect on the world of science – Homo erectus fossils aged twenty-seven thousand years were found on the island of Java. In the Kow swamp in Australia, some thirteen thousand year-old fossils were found that bore Homo Sapiens-Homo Erectus characteristics. All these fossils demonstrate that Homo erectus continued living up to times very close to our day and were nothing but a human race that has since been buried in history.

Archaic Homo Sapiens and Neanderthal Man

Archaic Homo sapiens is the immediate forerunner of contemporary man in the imaginary evolutionary scheme. In fact, evolutionists do not have much to say about these men, as there are only minor differences between them and modern men. Some researchers even state that representatives of this race are still living today, and point to the Aborigines in Australia as an example. Like Homo sapiens, the Aborigines also have thick protruding eyebrows, an inward-inclined mandibular structure, and a slightly smaller cranial volume. Moreover, significant discoveries have been made hinting that such people lived in Hungary and in some villages in Italy until not very long ago.

Evolutionists point to human fossils unearthed in the Neander valley of Holland which have been named Neanderthal Man. Many contemporary researchers define Neanderthal Man as a sub-species of modern man and call it "Homo sapiens neandertalensis". It is definite that this race lived together with modern humans, at the same time and in the same areas. The findings testify that Neanderthals buried their dead, fashioned musical instruments, and had cultural affinities with the Homo sapiens sapiens living during the same period. Entirely modern skulls and skeletal structures of Neanderthal fossils are not open to any speculation. A prominent authority on the subject, Erik Trinkaus from New Mexico University writes:

> Detailed comparisons of Neanderthal skeletal remains with those of modern humans have shown that there is nothing in Neanderthal anatomy that conclusively indicates locomotor, manipulative, intellectual, or linguistic abilities inferior to those of modern humans.[47]

In fact, Neanderthals even had some "evolutionary" advantages over modern men. The cranial capacity of Neanderthals was larger than that of the modern man and they were more robust and muscular than we are. Trinkaus adds: "One of the most characteristic features of the Neanderthals is the exaggerated massiveness of their trunk and limb bones. All of the preserved bones suggest a strength seldom attained by modern humans.

Furthermore, not only is this robustness present among the adult males, as one might expect, but it is also evident in the adult females, adolescents, and even children."

To put it precisely, Neanderthals are a particular human race that assimilated with other races in time.

All of these factors show that the scenario of "human evolution" fabricated by evolutionists is a figment of their imaginations, and that men have always been men and apes always apes.

Can Life Result from Coincidences as Revolution Argues?

The theory of evolution holds that life started with a cell that formed by chance under primitive earth conditions. Let us therefore examine the composition of the cell with simple comparisons in order to show how irrational it is to ascribe the existence of the cell – a structure which still maintains its mystery in many respects, even at a time when we are about to set foot in the 21st century – to natural phenomena and coincidences:

With all its operational systems, systems of communication, transportation and management, a cell is no less complex than any city. It contains power-stations producing the energy consumed by the cell, factories manufacturing the enzymes and hormones essential for life, a databank where all necessary information about all products to be produced is recorded, complex transportation systems and pipelines for carrying raw materials and products from one place to another, advanced laboratories and refineries for breaking down imported raw materials into their useable parts, and specialised cell membrane proteins for the control of in-coming and outgoing materials. These constitute only a small part of this incredibly complex system.

Far from being formed under primitive earth conditions, the cell, which in its composition and mechanisms is so complex, cannot be synthesised in even the most sophisticated laboratories of our day. Even with the use of amino acids, the building blocks of the cell, it is not possible to produce so much as a single organelle of the cell, such as mitochondria or ribosome, much less a whole cell. The first cell claimed to have been produced by evolutionary coincidence is as much a figment of the imagination and a product of fantasy as the unicorn.

Proteins Challenge Coincidence

And it is not just the cell that cannot be produced: the formation, under natural conditions, of even a single protein of the thousands of complex protein molecules making up a cell is impossible.

Proteins are giant molecules consisting of amino acids arranged in a particular sequence in certain quantities and structures. These molecules constitute the building blocks of a living cell. The simplest is composed of 50 amino acids; but there are some proteins that are composed of thousands of amino acids. The absence, addition, or replacement of a single amino acid in the structure of a protein in living cells, each of which has a particular function, causes the protein to become a useless molecular heap. Incapable of demonstrating the "accidental formation" of amino acids, the theory of evolution founders on the point of the formation of proteins.

We can easily demonstrate, with simple probability calculations anybody can understand, that the functional structure of proteins can by no means come about by chance.

There are twenty different amino acids. If we consider that an average-sized protein molecule is composed of 288 amino acids, there are 10^{300} different combinations of acids. Of all of these possible sequences, only "one" forms the desired protein molecule. The other amino-acid chains are either completely useless or else potentially harmful to living things. In other words, the probability of the coincidental formation of only one protein molecule cited above is "1 in 10^{300}". The probability of this "1" occurring out of an "astronomical" number consisting of 1 followed by 300 zeros is for all practical purposes zero; it is impossible. Furthermore, a protein molecule of 288 amino acids is rather a modest one compared with some giant protein molecules consisting of thousands of amino acids. When we apply similar probability calculations to these giant protein molecules, we see that even the word "impossible" becomes inadequate.

If the coincidental formation of even one of these proteins is impossible, it is billions of times more impossible for approximately one million of those proteins to come together by chance in an organised fashion and make up a complete human cell. Moreover, a cell is not merely a collection of proteins. In addition to proteins, cells also include nucleic acids, carbohydrates, lipids, vitamins, and many other chemicals such as electrolytes, all of which are arranged harmoniously and with design in specific proportions, both in terms of structure and function. Each functions as a building block or component in various organelles.

As we have seen, evolution is unable to explain the formation of even a single protein out of the millions in the cell, let alone explain the cell.

Prof. Dr. Ali Demirsoy, one of the foremost authorities of evolutionist thought in Turkey, in his book *Kalitim ve Evrim* (Inheritance and Evolution), discusses the probability of the accidental formation of Cytochrome-C, one of the essential enzymes for life:

> The probability of the formation of a Cytochrome-C sequence is as likely as zero. That is, if life requires a certain sequence, it can be said that this has a probability likely to be realised once in the whole universe. Otherwise, some metaphysical powers beyond our definition should have acted in its formation. To accept the latter is not appropriate to the goals of science. We therefore have to look into the first hypothesis.[48]

After these lines, Demirsoy admits that this probability, which he accepted just because it was "more appropriate to the goals of science", is unrealistic:

> The probability of providing the particular amino acid sequence of Cytochrome-C is as unlikely as the possibility of a monkey writing the history of humanity on a typewriter – taking it for granted that the monkey pushes the keys at random.[49]

The correct sequence of proper amino acids is simply not enough for the formation of one of the protein molecules present in living things. Besides this, each of the twenty different types of amino acid present in the composition of proteins must be left-handed. Chemically, there are two different types of amino acids called "left-handed" and "right-handed". The difference between them is the mirror-symmetry between their three dimensional structures, which is similar to that of a person's right and left hands. Amino acids of either of these two types are found in equal numbers in nature and they can bond perfectly well with one another. Yet, research uncovers an astonishing fact: all proteins present in the structure of living things are made up of left-handed amino acids. Even a single right-handed amino acid attached to the structure of a protein renders it useless.

Let us for an instant suppose that life came into existence by chance as evolutionists claim. In this case, the right and left-handed amino acids that were generated by chance should be present in nature in roughly equal amounts. The question of how proteins can pick out only left-handed amino acids, and how not even a single right-handed amino acid becomes involved in the life process is something that still confounds evolutionists. In the *Britannica Science Encyclopaedia*, an ardent defender of evolution, the authors indicate that the amino acids of all living organisms on earth and the building blocks of complex polymers such as proteins have the same left-handed asymmetry. They add that this is tantamount to tossing a coin a million times and always getting heads. In the same encyclopaedia, they state that it is not possible to understand why molecules become left-handed or right-handed and that this choice is fascinatingly related to the source of life on earth.[50]

It is not enough for amino acids to be arranged in the correct numbers, sequences, and in the required three-dimensional structures. The formation of a protein also requires that amino acid molecules with more than one arm be linked to each other only through certain arms. Such a bond is called a "peptide bond". Amino acids can make different bonds with each other; but proteins comprise those and only those amino acids that join together by "peptide" bonds.

Research has shown that only 50 % of amino acids, combining at random, combine with a peptide bond and that the rest combine with different bonds that are not present in proteins. To function properly, each amino acid making up a protein must join with other amino acids with a peptide bond, as it has only to be chosen from among the left-handed

The probability of an average protein molecule comprising five hundred amino acids being arranged in the correct proportion and sequence in addition to the probability of all of the amino acids it contains being only left-handed and being combined only with peptide bonds is "1" divided by 10^{950}. We can write this number, which is formed by putting 950 zeros after 1, as follows:

$$10^{950} =$$

100,000,000,000,000,000,000,000,000,000,000,000,000,000,000,000,000,
000,000,000,000,000,000,000,000,000,000,000,000,000,000,000,000,000,
000,000,000,000,000,000,000,000,000,000,000,000,000,000,000,000,000,
000,000,000,000,000,000,000,000,000,000,000,000,000,000,000,000,000,
000,000,000,000,000,000,000,000,000,000,000,000,000,000,000,000,000,
000,000,000,000,000,000,000,000,000,000,000,000,000,000,000,000,000,
000,000,000,000,000,000,000,000,000,000,000,000,000,000,000,000,000,
000,000,000,000,000,000,000,000,000,000,000,000,000,000,000,000,000,
000,000,000,000,000,000,000,000,000,000,000,000,000,000,000,000,000,
000,000,000,000,000,000,000,000,000,000,000,000,000,000,000,000,000,
000,000,000,000,000,000,000,000,000,000,000,000,000,000,000,000,000,
000,000,000,000,000,000,000,000,000,000,000,000,000,000,000,000,000,
000,000,000,000,000,000,000,000,000,000,000,000,000,000,000,000,000,
000,000,000,000,000,000,000,000,000,000,000,000,000,000,000,000,000,
000,000,000,000,000,000,000,000,000,000,000,000,000,000,000,000,000,
000,000,000,000,000,000,000,000,000,000,000,000,000,000,000,000,000,
000,000,000,000,000,000,000,000,000,000,000,000

ones. Unquestionably, there is no control mechanism to select and leave out the right-handed amino acids and personally make sure that each amino acid makes a peptide bond with the other.

Under these circumstances, the probabilities of an average protein molecule comprising five hundred amino acids arranging itself in the correct quantities and in sequence, in addition to the probabilities of all of the amino acids it contains being only left-handed and combining using only peptide bonds are as follows:

– The probability of being in the right sequence $= 1/20^{500} = 1/10^{650}$
– The probability of being left-handed $= 1/2^{500} = 1/10^{150}$
– The probability of combining using a "peptide bond" $= 1/2^{499} = 1/10^{150}$

TOTAL PROBABILITY $= 1/10^{950}$ that is, **"1" probability in 10^{950}**

As you can see above, the probability of the formation of a protein molecule comprising five hundred amino acids is "1" divided by a number formed by placing 950 zeros after a 1, a number incomprehensible to the human mind. This is only a probability on paper. Practically, such a possibility has "0" chance of realisation. In mathematics, a probability smaller than 1 over 10^{50} is statistically considered to have a "0" probability of realisation.

While the improbability of the formation of a protein molecule made up of five hundred amino acids reaches such an extent, we can further proceed to push the limits of the mind to higher levels of improbability. In the "haemoglobin" molecule, a vital protein, there are five hundred and seventy-four amino acids, which is a much larger number than that of the amino acids making up the protein mentioned above. Now consider this: in only one out of the billions of red blood cells in your body, there are "280,000,000" (280 million) haemoglobin molecules. The supposed age of the earth is not sufficient to afford the formation of even a single protein, let alone a red blood cell, by the method of "trial and error". The conclusion from all this is that evolution falls into a terrible abyss of improbability right at the stage of the formation of a single protein.

Looking for Answers to the Generation of Life

Well aware of the terrible odds against the possibility of life forming by chance, evolutionists were unable to provide a rational explanation for their beliefs so they set about looking for ways to demonstrate that the odds were not so unfavourable.

They designed a number of laboratory experiments to address the question of how life could generate itself from non-living matter. The best known and most respected of these experiments is the one known as the "Miller Experiment" or "Urey-Miller Experiment", which was conducted by the American researcher Stanley Miller in 1953.

With the purpose of proving that amino acids could have come into existence by accident, Miller created an atmosphere in his laboratory that he assumed would have existed on primordial earth (but which later proved to be unrealistic) and he set to work. The mixture he used for this primordial atmosphere was composed of ammonia, methane, hydrogen, and water vapour.

Miller knew that methane, ammonia, water vapour and hydrogen would not react with each other under natural conditions. He was aware that he had to inject energy into the mixture to start a reaction. He suggested that this energy could have come from lightning flashes in the primordial atmosphere and, relying on this supposition, he used an artificial electricity discharge in his experiments.

Miller boiled this gas mixture at 100 ^{0}C for a week, and, in addition, he introduced an electric current into the chamber. At the end of the week, Miller analysed the chemicals that had been formed in the chamber and observed that three of the twenty amino acids, which constitute the basic elements of proteins, had been synthesised.

This experiment aroused great excitement among evolutionists and they promoted it as an outstanding success. Encouraged by the thought that this experiment definitely verified their theory, evolutionists immediately produced new scenarios. Miller had supposedly proved that amino acids could form by themselves. Relying on this, they hurriedly hypothesised the following stages. According to their scenario, amino acids had later by accident united in the proper sequences to form proteins. Some of these accidentally formed proteins placed themselves in cell membrane-like structures, which "somehow" came into existence and formed a primitive cell. The cells united in time and formed living organisms. The greatest mainstay of the scenario was Miller's experiment.

However, Miller's experiment was nothing but make-believe, and has since been proven invalid in many respects.

The Invalidity of Miller's Experiment

Nearly half a century has passed since Miller conducted his experiment. Although it has been shown to be invalid in many respects, evolutionists still advance Miller and his results as absolute proof that life could have formed spontaneously from non-living matter. When we assess Miller's experiment critically, without the bias and subjectivity of evolutionist thinking, however, it is evident that the situation is not as rosy as evolutionists would have us think. Miller set for himself the goal of proving that amino acids could form by themselves in earth's primitive conditions. Some amino acids were produced but the conduct of the experiment conflicts with his goal in many ways, as we shall now see.

✦ Miller isolated the amino acids from the environment as soon as they were formed, by using a mechanism called a "cold trap". Had he not done so, the conditions of the environment in which the amino acids formed would immediately have destroyed the molecules.

It is quite meaningless to suppose that some conscious mechanism of this sort was integral to earth's primordial conditions, which involved ultraviolet radiation, thunderbolts, various chemicals, and a high percentage of free oxygen. Without such a mechanism, any amino acid that did manage to form would immediately have been destroyed.

✦ The primordial atmospheric environment that Miller attempted to simulate in his experiment was not realistic. Nitrogen and carbon dioxide would have been constituents of the primordial atmosphere, but Miller disregarded this and used methane and ammonia instead.

Why? Why were evolutionists insistent on the point that the primitive atmosphere contained high amounts of methane (CH_4), ammonia (NH_3), and water vapour (H_2O)? The answer is simple: without ammonia, it is impossible to synthesise an amino acid. Kevin McKean talks about this in an article published in *Discover* magazine:

> Miller and Urey imitated the ancient atmosphere of earth with a mixture of methane and ammonia. According to them, the earth was a true homogeneous mixture of metal, rock and ice. However in the latest studies, it is understood that the earth was very hot at those times and that it was composed of melted nickel and iron. Therefore, the chemical atmosphere of that time should have been formed mostly of nitrogen (N_2), carbon dioxide (CO_2) and water vapour (H_2O). However these are not as appropriate as methane and ammonia for the production of organic molecules.[51]

After a long period of silence, Miller himself also confessed that the atmospheric environment he used in his experiment was not realistic.

✦ Another important point invalidating Miller's experiment is that there was enough oxygen to destroy all the amino acids in the atmosphere at the time when evolutionists thought that amino acids formed. This oxygen concentration would definitely have hindered the formation of amino acids. This situation completely negates Miller's experiment, in which he totally neglected oxygen. If he had used oxygen in the experiment, methane would have decomposed into carbon dioxide and water, and ammonia would have decomposed into nitrogen and water.

On the other hand, since no ozone layer yet existed, no organic molecule could possibly have lived on earth because it was entirely unprotected against intense ultraviolet rays.

✦ In addition to a few amino acids essential for life, Miller's experiment also produced many organic acids with characteristics that are quite detrimental to the structures and functions of living things. If he had not isolated the amino acids and had left them in the same environment with these chemicals, their destruction or transformation into different compounds through chemical reactions would have been unavoidable. Moreover, a large number of right-handed amino acids also formed. The existence of these amino acids alone refuted the theory, even within its own reasoning, because right-handed amino acids are unable to function in the composition of living organisms and render proteins useless when they are involved in their composition.

To conclude, the circumstances in which amino acids formed in Miller's experiment were not suitable for life forms to come into being. The medium in which they formed was an acidic mixture that destroyed and oxidised any useful molecules that might have been obtained.

Evolutionists themselves actually refute the theory of evolution, as they are often wont to do, by advancing this experiment as "proof". If the experiment proves anything, it is that amino acids can only be produced in a controlled laboratory environment where all the necessary conditions have been specifically and consciously designed. That is, the experiment shows that what brings life (even the "near-life" of amino acids) into being cannot be unconscious chance, but rather conscious will – in a word, Creation. This is why every stage of Creation is a sign proving to us the existence and might of Allah.

The Miraculous Molecule: DNA

The theory of evolution has been unable to provide a coherent explanation for the existence of the molecules that are the basis of the cell. Furthermore, developments in the science of genetics and the discovery of the nucleic acids (DNA and RNA) have produced brand-new problems for the theory of evolution.

In 1955, the work of two scientists on DNA, James Watson and Francis Crick, launched a new era in biology. Many scientists directed their attention to the science of genetics. Today, after years of research, scientists have, largely, mapped the structure of DNA.

Here, we need to give some very basic information on the structure and function of DNA:

The molecule called DNA, which exists in the nucleus of each of the 100 trillion cells in our body, contains the complete construction plan of the human body. Information regarding all the characteristics of a person, from the physical appearance to the structure of the inner organs, is recorded in DNA by means of a special coding system. The information in DNA is coded within the sequence of four special bases that make up this molecule. These bases are specified as A, T, G, and C according to the initial letters of their names. All the structural differences among people depend on the variations in the sequence of these bases. There are approximately 3.5 billion nucleotides, that is, 3.5 billion letters in a DNA molecule.

The DNA data pertaining to a particular organ or protein is included in special components called "genes". For instance, information about the eye exists in a series of special genes, whereas information about the heart exists in quite another series of genes. The cell produces proteins by using the information in all of these genes. Amino acids that constitute the structure of the protein are defined by the sequential arrangement of three nucleotides in the DNA.

At this point, an important detail deserves attention. An error in the sequence of nucleotides making up a gene renders the gene completely useless. When we consider that there are 200 thousand genes in the human

The molecule called DNA contains the complete construction plan of the human body.

body, it becomes more evident how impossible it is for the millions of nucleotides making up these genes to form by accident in the right sequence. An evolutionist biologist, Frank Salisbury, comments on this impossibility by saying:

> A medium protein might include about 300 amino acids. The DNA gene controlling this would have about 1,000 nucleotides in its chain. Since there are four kinds of nucleotides in a DNA chain, one consisting of 1,000 links could exist in 4^{1000} forms. Using a little algebra (logarithms), we can see that $4^{1000}=10^{600}$. Ten multiplied by itself 600 times gives the figure 1 followed by 600 zeros! This number is completely beyond our comprehension.[52]

The number 4^{1000} is equivalent to 10^{600}. We obtain this number by adding 600 zeros to 1. As 10 with 11 zeros indicates a trillion, a figure with 600 zeros is indeed a number that is difficult to grasp.

Evolutionist Prof. Ali Demirsoy was forced to make the following admission on this issue:

> In fact, the probability of the random formation of a protein and a nucleic

acid (DNA-RNA) is inconceivably small. The chances against the emergence of even a particular protein chain are astronomic.[53]

In addition to all these improbabilities, DNA can barely be involved in a reaction because of its double-chained spiral shape. This also makes it impossible to think that it can be the basis of life.

Moreover, while DNA can replicate only with the help of some enzymes that are actually proteins, the synthesis of these enzymes can be realised only by the information coded in DNA. As they both depend on each other, either they have to exist at the same time for replication, or one of them has had to be "created" before the other. American microbiologist Jacobson comments on the subject:

> The complete directions for the reproduction of plans, for energy and the extraction of parts from the current environment, for the growth sequence, and for the effector mechanism translating instructions into growth – all had to be simultaneously present at that moment (when life began). This combination of events has seemed an incredibly unlikely happenstance, and has often been ascribed to divine intervention.[54]

The quotation above was written two years after the disclosure of the structure of DNA by James Watson and Francis Crick. Despite all the developments in science, this problem remains unsolved for evolutionists. To sum up, the need for DNA in reproduction, the necessity of the presence of some proteins for reproduction, and the requirement to produce these proteins according to the information in the DNA entirely demolish evolutionist theses.

Two German scientists, Junker and Scherer, explained that the synthesis of each of the molecules required for chemical evolution, necessitates distinct conditions, and that the probability of the compounding of these materials having theoretically very different acquirement methods is zero:

> Until now, no experiment is known in which we can obtain all the molecules necessary for chemical evolution. Therefore, it is essential to produce various molecules in different places under very suitable conditions and then to carry them to another place for reaction by protecting them from harmful elements like hydrolysis and photolysis.[55]

In short, the theory of evolution is unable to prove any of the evolutionary stages that allegedly occur at the molecular level.

To summarise what we have said so far, neither amino acids nor their products, the proteins making up the cells of living beings, could ever be produced in any so-called "primitive atmosphere" environment. Moreover, factors such as the incredibly complex structure of proteins, their right-hand, left-hand features, and the difficulties in the formation of peptide bonds are just parts of the reason why they will never be produced in any future experiment either.

Even if we suppose for a moment that proteins somehow did form accidentally, that would still have no meaning, for proteins are nothing at all on their own: they cannot themselves reproduce. Protein synthesis is only possible with the information coded in DNA and RNA molecules. Without DNA and RNA, it is impossible for a protein to reproduce. The specific sequence of the twenty different amino acids encoded in DNA determines the structure of each protein in the body. However, as has been made abundantly clear by all those who have studied these molecules, it is impossible for DNA and RNA to form by chance.

The Fact of Creation

With the collapse of the theory of evolution in every field, prominent names in the discipline of microbiology today admit the fact of creation and have begun to defend the view that everything is created by a conscious Creator as part of an exalted creation. This is already a fact that people cannot disregard. Scientists who can approach their work with an open mind have developed a view called "intelligent design". Michael J. Behe, one of the foremost of these scientists, states that he accepts the absolute being of the Creator and describes the impasse of those who deny this fact:

> The result of these cumulative efforts to investigate the cell – to investigate life at the molecular level – is a loud, clear, piercing cry of "design!" The result is so unambiguous and so significant that it must be ranked as one of the greatest achievements in the history of science. This triumph of science should evoke cries of "Eureka" from ten thousand throats.

> But, no bottles have been uncorked, no hands clapped. Instead, a curious, embarrassed silence surrounds the stark complexity of the cell. When the

subject comes up in public, feet start to shuffle, and breathing gets a bit laboured. In private people are a bit more relaxed; many explicitly admit the obvious but then stare at the ground, shake their heads, and let it go like that. Why does the scientific community not greedily embrace its startling discovery? Why is the observation of design handled with intellectual gloves? The dilemma is that while one side of the [issue] is labelled intelligent design, the other side must be labelled God.[56]

Today, many people are not even aware that they are in a position of accepting a body of fallacy as truth in the name of science, instead of believing in Allah. Those who do not find the sentence "Allah created you from nothing" scientific enough can believe that the first living being came into being by thunderbolts striking a "primordial soup" billions of years ago.

As we have described elsewhere in this book, the balances in nature are so delicate and so numerous that it is entirely irrational to claim that they developed "by chance". No matter how much those who cannot set themselves free from this irrationality may strive, the signs of Allah in the heavens and the earth are completely obvious and they are undeniable.

Allah is the Creator of the heavens, the earth and all that is between.

The signs of His being have encompassed the entire universe.

Glory to You, of knowledge We have
none, save what You have taught us:
In truth it is You Who is perfect in
knowledge and wisdom.
(Surat al-Baqara, 32)

NOTES

1. A. Maton, J. Hopkins, S. Johnson, D. LaHart, M.Quon Warner, J.D. Wright, *Human Biology and Health*, Prentice Hall, New Jersey, p. 59

2. J.A.C. Brown, *Medical and Health Encyclopaedia*, Remzi Publishing, Istanbul, p.250

3. H.J. de Blij, M.H. Glantz, S.L. Harris, *Restless Earth*, The National Geographic Society, 1997, p.8

4. H.J. de Blij, M.H. Glantz, S.L. Harris, *Restless Earth*, The National Geographic Society, 1997, p.8

5. H.J. de Blij, M.H. Glantz, S.L. Harris, *Restless Earth*, The National Geographic Society, 1997, p. 64

6. H.J. de Blij, M.H. Glantz, S.L. Harris, *Restless Earth*, The National Geographic Society, 1997, p.18-19

7. H.J. de Blij, M.H. Glantz, S.L. Harris, *Restless Earth*, The National Geographic Society, 1997, p.64

8. The Guinness Book of Amazing Nature, p.60

9. H.J. de Blij, M.H. Glantz, S.L. Harris, *Restless Earth*, The National Geographic Society, 1997, p.105

10. *National Geographic*, July 1988, p.29

11. Mesopotamia and Ancient Near East, *Great Civilisations Encyclopaedia*, Iletisim Publications, p.92

12. *Ana Brittannica*, Volume 20, p.592

13. H.J. de Blij, M.H. Glantz, S.L. Harris, *Restless Earth*, The National Geographic Society, 1997, p.18-19

14. Frederick Vester, *Denken, Lernen, Vergessen*, vga, 1978, p.6

15. George Politzer, *Principes Fondamentaux de Philosophie*, Editions Sociales, Paris 1954, pp.38-39-44

16. R.L.Gregory, *Eye and Brain: The Psychology of Seeing*, Oxford University Press Inc. New York, 1990, p.9

17. Lincoln Barnett, *The Universe and Dr.Einstein*, William Sloane Associate, New York, 1948, p.20

18. Orhan Hancerlioglu, *Dusunce Tarihi (The History of Thought)*, Istanbul: Remzi Bookstore, 6.ed., 1995 September, p. 447

19. George Berkeley, *A Treatise Concerning The Principles of Human Knowledge*, 1710, Works of George Berkeley, vol. I, ed. A. Fraser, Oxford, 1871

20. Bertrand Russell, *ABC of Relativity*, George Allen and Unwin, London, 1964, p. 161-162

21. R.L.Gregory, *Eye and Brain: The Psychology of Seeing*, Oxford University Press Inc. New York, 1990, p.9

22. Ken Wilber, *Holographic Paradigm and Other Paradoxes*, p.20

23. George Politzer, *Principes Fondamentaux de Philosophie*, Editions Sociales, Paris 1954, p. 65.

24. Orhan Hancerlioglu, *Dusunce Tarihi (The History of Thought)*, Istanbul: Remzi Bookstore, 6.ed., 1995 September, p. 261

25. George Politzer, *Principes Fondamentaux de Philosophie*, Editions Sociales, Paris 1954, pp.65

26. David Hume, *A Treatise of Human Nature*, Book I, Section IV: Of Personal Identity

27. Rennan Pekunlu, "Aldatmacanin Evrimsizligi", (Non-Evolution of Deceit), *Bilim ve Utopya*, December 1998, (V.I. Lenin, Materialism and Empiriocriticism, Progress Publishers, Moscow, 1970, p.334-335)

28. Alaettin Senel, "Evrim Aldatmacasi mi? Devrin Aldatmacasi mi?", (Non-Evolution of Deceit), *Bilim ve Utopya*, December 1998

29. *Mektubat-i Rabbani (Letters of Rabbani)*, Vol II, 357. Letter, p. 163.

30. *Mektubat-i Rabbani (Letters of Rabbani)*, Vol II, 357. Letter, p. 1432

31. François Jacob, *Le Jeu des Possibles*, University of Washington Press, 1982, p. 111

32. Lincoln Barnett, *The Universe and Dr. Einstein*, William Sloane Associate, New York, 1948, pp. 39-40.

33. Lincoln Barnett, *The Universe and Dr. Einstein*, p. 12.

34. Lincoln Barnett, *The Universe and Dr. Einstein*, p. 40.

35. Paul Strathern, *The Big Idea: Einstein and Relativity*, Arrow Books, 1997, p. 57

36. Lincoln Barnett, *The Universe and Dr. Einstein*, p. 67.

37. Lincoln Barnett, *The Universe and Dr. Einstein*, p.12.

38. Charles Darwin, *The Origin of Species: A Facsimile of the First Edition*, Harvard University Press, 1964, p. 189.

39. Derek A. Ager. "The Nature of the Fossil Record". *Proceedings of the British Geological Association*, vol. 87, no. 2, (1976), p. 133.

40. T.N. George, "Fossils in Evolutionary Perspective", *Science Progress*, vol.48, (January 1960), p.1-3

41. Richard Monestarsky, "Mysteries of the Orient", *Discover*, April 1993, p.40.

42. Stefan Bengston, *Nature* 345:765 (1990).

43. Earnest A. Hooton, *Up From The Ape*, New York: McMillan, 1931, p.332.

44. Stephen Jay Gould, "Smith Woodward's Folly", *New Scientist*, 5 April 1979, p. 44.

45. Charles E. Oxnard, The Place of Australopithecines in Human Evolution: Grounds for Doubt, *Natura*, No. 258, p. 389.

46. Richard Leakey, *The Making of Mankind*, London: Sphere Books 1981, p. 116

47. Eric Trinkaus, Hard Times Among the Neanderthals, *Natural History*, No. 87, December 1978, p. 10, R.L. Holoway, "The Neanderthal Brain: What was Primitive?", *American Journal of Physical Anthropology Supplement*, No. 12, 1991, p. 94

48. Ali Demirsoy, *Kalitim ve Evrim (Inheritance and Evolution)*, Ankara: Meteksan Yayinlari 1984, p. 61

49. Ibid.

50. *Fabbri Britannica Science Encyclopaedia*, Vol. 2, No. 22, p. 519

51. Kevin McKean, No. 189, p. 7

52. Frank B. Salisbury, "Doubts about the Modern Synthetic Theory of Evolution", *American Biology Teacher*, September 1971, p. 336.

53. Ali Demirsoy, *Kalitim ve Evrim (Inheritance and Evolution)*, Ankara: Meteksan Publishing Co., 1984, p. 39.

54. Homer Jacobson, "Information, Reproduction and the Origin of Life", *American Scientist*, January 1955, p.121.

55. Reinhard Junker & Siegfried Scherer, "Entstehung Gesiche Der Lebewesen", Weyel, 1986, p. 89

56. Michael J. Behe, *Darwin's Black Box*, New York: Free Press, 1996, pp. 232-233.

Many people think that Darwin's Theory of Evolution is a proven fact. Contrary to this conventional wisdom, recent developments in science completely disprove the theory. The only reason Darwinism is still foisted on people by means of a world-wide propaganda campaign lies in the ideological aspects of the theory. All secular ideologies and philosophies try to provide a basis for themselves by relying on the theory of evolution.

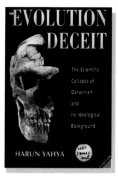

This book clarifies the scientific collapse of the theory of evolution in a way that is detailed but easy to understand. It reveals the frauds and distortions committed by evolutionists to "prove" evolution. Finally it analyzes the powers and motives that strive to keep this theory alive and make people believe in it.

Anyone who wants to learn about the origin of living things, including mankind, needs to read this book.

238 PAGES WITH 166 PICTURES IN COLOUR

One of the purposes why the Qur'an was revealed is to summon people to think about creation and its works. When a person examines his own body or any other living thing in nature, the world or the whole universe, in it he sees a great design, art, plan and intelligence. All this is evidence proving Allah's being, unit, and eternal power.

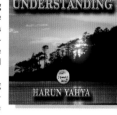

For Men of Understanding was written to make the reader see and realise some of the evidence of creation in nature. Many living miracles are revealed in the book with hundreds of pictures and brief explanations.

288 PAGES WITH 467 PICTURES IN COLOUR

Many societies that rebelled against the will of God or regarded His messengers as enemies were wiped off the face of the earth completely... Perished Nations examines these penalties as revealed in the verses of the Quran and in light of archaeological discoveries. This book is also available in German, French, Spanish, Russian and Portuguese.

149 PAGES WITH 73 PICTURES IN COLOUR

The evidence of Allah's creation is present everywhere in the universe. A person comes across many of these proofs in the course of his daily life; yet if he does not think deeply, he may wrongly á These aspects of ants create in one a great admiration for Allah's superior power and unmatched creation.

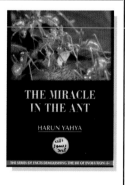

165 PAGES WITH 104 PICTURES IN COLOUR

One of the major reasons why people feel a profound sense of attachment to life and cast religion aside is the assumption that life is eternal. Forgetting that death is likely to put an end to this life at any time, man simply believes that he can enjoy a perfect and happy life. Yet he evidently deceives himself. The world is a temporary place specially created by Allah to

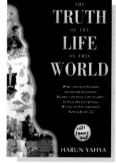

test man. That is why, it is inherently flawed and far from satisfying man's endless needs and desires. Each and every attraction existing in the world eventually wears out, becomes corrupt, decays and finally disappears. This is the never-changing reality of life.

This book explains this most important essence of life and leads man to ponder the real place to which he belongs, namely the Hereafter.

224 PAGES WITH 144 PICTURES IN COLOUR

In a body that is made up of atoms, you breathe in air, eat food, and drink liquids that are all composed of atoms. Everything you see is nothing but the result of the collision of electrons of atoms with photons.

In this book, the implausibility of the spontaneous formation of an atom, the building-block of everything, living or non-living, is related and the flawless nature of Allah's creation is demonstrated.

139 PAGES WITH 122 PICTURES IN COLOUR

In the Qur'an, there is an explicit reference to the "second coming of the Jesus to the world" which is heralded in a hadith. The realisation of some information revealed in the Qur'an about Jesus can only be possible by Jesus' second coming...

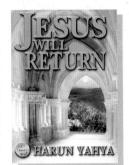

102 PAGES

People who are oppressed, who are tortured to death, innocent babies, those who cannot afford even a loaf of bread, who must sleep in tents or even in streets in cold weather, those who are massacred just because they belong to a certain tribe, women, children, and old people who are expelled from their homes because of their religion... Eventually, there is only one solution to the injustice, chaos, terror, massacres, hunger, poverty, and oppression: the morals of the Qur'an.

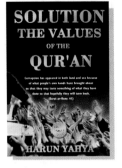

208 PAGES WITH 276 PICTURES IN COLOUR

Darwin said: "If it could be demonstrated that any complex organ existed, which could not possibly have been formed by numerous, successive, slight modifications, my theory would absolutely break down." When you read this book, you will see that Darwin's theory has absolutely broken down, just as he feared it would.

208 PAGES WITH 302 PICTURES IN COLOUR

Have you ever thought that you were non-existent before you were born and suddenly appeared on Earth? Have you ever thought that the peel of a banana, melon, watermelon or an orange each serve as a quality package preserving the fruit's odour and taste?

Man is a being to which Allah has granted the faculty of thinking. Yet a majority of people fail to employ this faculty as they should... The purpose of this book is to summon people to think in the way they should and to guide them in their efforts to think.

128 PAGES WITH 137 PICTURES IN COLOUR

Colours, patterns, spots even lines of each living being existing in nature have a meaning. For some species, colours serve as a communication tool; for others, they are a warning against enemies. Whatever the case, these colours are essential for the well-being of living beings. An attentive eye would immediately recognise that not only the living beings, but also everything in nature are just as they should be. Furthermore, he would realise that everything is given to the service of man: the comforting blue colour of the sky, the colourful view of flowers, the bright green trees and meadows, the moon and stars illuminating the world in pitch darkness together with innumerable beauties surrounding man...

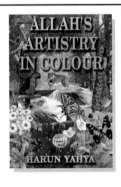

160 PAGES WITH 215 PICTURES IN COLOUR

Never plead ignorance of Allah's evident existence, that everything was created by Allah, that everything you own was given to you by Allah for your subsistence, that you will not stay so long in this world, of the reality of death, that the Qur'an is the Book of truth, that you will give account for your deeds, of the voice of your conscience that always invites you to righteousness, of the existence of the hereafter and the day of account, that hell is the eternal home of severe punishment, and of the reality of fate.

112 PAGES WITH 74 PICTURES IN COLOUR

CHILDREN'S BOOKS

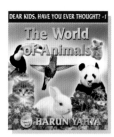

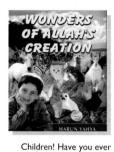

Dear children, while reading this book, you will see how Allah has created all the creatures in the most beautiful way and how every one of them show us His endless beauty, power and knowledge.
136 PAGES WITH 200 PICTURES IN COLOUR

Dear children, while reading this book, you will see how Allah has created all the creatures in the most beautiful way and how every one of them show us His endless beauty, power and knowledge.
136 PAGES WITH 200 PICTURES IN COLOUR

Have you ever thought about the vast dimensions of the universe we live in? As you read this book, you will see that our universe and all the living things therein are created in the most perfect way by our Creator, Allah.
136 PAGES WITH 198 PICTURES IN COLOUR

Children! Have you ever asked yourself questions like these: How did our earth come into existence? Where were you before you were born? How did oceans, trees, animals appear on earth? Who was the first human being? In this book you will find the true answers to these questions.
144 PAGES WITH 282 PICTURES IN COLOUR

MEDIA PRODUCTS BASED ON THE WORKS OF HARUN YAHYA

Audio cassettes based on the works of Harun Yahya include The Collapse of the "Theory of Evolution-The Fact of Creation", "The Creation of the Universe-The Balances in the Earth", "The Miracle in the Cell-The Miracle of Birth", "The Miracle in the Eye-The Miracle in the Ear", "The Design in Animals-The Design in Plants", "The Miracle in the Honeybee-The Miracle in the Ant", "The Miracle in the Mosquito-The Miracle in the Spider", "Self-Sacrifice in Living Things-Migration and Orientation", "The Miracle of Creation in DNA", "Miracles of the Qur'an".

HARUN YAHYA ON THE INTERNET

ON THE NEWS Our ONLINE BOOKSTORE is launched. You can order all Harun Yahya books and videos from any country in the world.

HARUN YAHYA
AN INVITATION TO THE TRUTH

SEARCH [GO] ABOUT THIS SITE CONTACT US HOME LANGUAGE [English]

AUTHOR
Who is Harun Yahya?

BOOKS
Full Texts Available ▶

ARTICLES
of Science and Faith ▶

VIDEO
Documentaries On-line ▶

AUDIO
Recordings On-line ▶

All Downloads

Ordering

A Call to All Translators, Publishers & Distributors
COME & WORK WITH US

ISLAM DENOUNCES TERRORISM.com

VISIT OUR NEW SITE

EXHIBITION
A Visual Gallery of Creation

Subscribe
Subscribe for our free newsletters

HARUN YAHYA'S Best Seller
EVOLUTION DECEIT
Now in 7 different languages
Bosnian

Featured Sites

SCIENTIFIC AMERICAN'S 15 ERRORS

The July issue of Scientific American magazine carried a misleading article titled "15 Answers to Creationist Nonsense," which actually contained no true answers at all, but merely consisted of Darwinist dogmatism. **NEW**

ALSO READ: New skull fossil sinks evolutionary theories

THE FACT OF CREATION

Every creature is evidence of the Creator. In the books of Harun Yahya, you will discover the creative art, wisdom and power of God.

TRUE ISLAMIC MORALS

Islam is the last divine religion revealed to mankind. It is the true path that leads us to God. It is also the basis for moral values like justice, modesty, mercy and love. Read about the Islamic morals in the books of Harun Yahya and discover a whole new world.

Jesus will Return

Jesus will return to the world for a second time. He will unite all believers in God and bring peace to mankind, as proclaimed by the Prophet Mohammad and revealed in the Qur'an.

The Two Great Deceptions:
DARWINISM & MATERIALISM

The dogmas of materialism and Darwinism has mislead the world since the 19th century. But now science is shattering these myths. Learn how...

PERISHED NATIONS

Many ancient societies were destroyed because they rebelled against God. Learn their true stories from the Qur'an and the archaeological evidence...

THE TRUTH OF THE WORLDLY LIFE

Have you ever wondered why we age, get sick and eventually die? Why our lives never satisfy us? Discover the deep meaning of the life of this world.

FEATURED BOOK
ALLAH'S ARTISTRY IN COLOUR
HARUN YAHYA

TAKE A TOUR
On The COLLAPSE of EVOLUTION
An Audio-Visual Presentation

QUIZ of the DAY
Why are the "ape men" drawings in the media nothing but pure imagination?

CLICK TO LEARN

▶ Worldwide
The global impact of Harun Yahya's works

▶ Catalog
The complete Harun Yahya collection in all languages

▶ Comments
Opinions of readers around the World

▶ Quotes
Selected quotes from Harun Yahya writings

TRUTHS for KIDS

e-mail ≫ this site to a friend

NEW RELEASES: All Free to Read & Download

- Romanticism: A Weapon of Satan
- The Prophet Musa (AS)
- Basic Tenets of Islam
- The Miracle of Creation in Plants
- Fascism: The Bloody Ideology of Darwinism
- Death Resurrection Hell
- The Design in Nature
- The Qur'an Leads the Way to Science
- The Alliance of The Good
- The Complete Works of Harun Yahya
- Some Secrets of the Qur'an
- Islam Denounces Terrorism

YOU CAN FIND ALL THE WORKS OF HARUN YAHYA ON THE INTERNET

- Scientific refutation of Darwinism, the greatest deception of our age.
- Dozens of books including hundreds of pages of information about the signs of God's creation.
- Extremely valuable works that will guide you to think on the real aspects of life by reading the morals of the Qur'an.
- Harun Yahya's political, scientific and faith-related articles that have appeared in various magazines and newspapers around the world.
- Audio recordings and documentary videos inspired by the works of Harun Yahya.
- And many more attractive presentations...

www.harunyahya.com - www.hyahya.org - e-mail: info@harunyahya.com